Life Changing Journey

500 Inspirational Quotes

SERIES VII

"Unveiling Wisdom: Inspiring Quotes to Spark Your Life. A Treasury of Inspiration for Cultivating Positivity on Life, Love, Nature, and More."

SHREE SHAMBAV

AF517503

Life Changing Journey

Shree Shambav

Published by Shree Shambav, Tamil Nadu, India
Shree Shambav Ink & Imagination "Where Words Breathe and Imagination Soars"
All Rights Reserved

First Edition, 2025

Copyright © 2025, Muniswamy Rajakumar

All rights reserved. No part of this publication may be reproduced, distributed, or transmitted in any form or by any means, including photocopying, recording, or other electronic or mechanical methods, without the author's prior written permission. It is illegal to copy this book, post it to a website, or distribute it by any other means without permission.

The request for permission should be addressed to the author.

Email: shreeshambav@gmail.com

Web: www.shambav.org

DEDICATION

"Isavasyam idam sarvam yat kim ca jagatyam jagat, tena tyaktena bhunjitha, ma gridhah kasyasvid dhanam"

To the Almighty,

the Divine Masters,

the family who listens,

and my parents who see –

your presence shapes the pages of my life's journey.

"Isavasyam idam sarvam yat kim ca jagatyam jagat"

Meaning: "God encompasses everything you perceive, see, or touch with your sense organs."

DISCLAIMER

This book, *"Life-Changing Journey - Inspirational Quotes: Series VII,"* is a heartfelt compilation of personal reflections and insights born from the author's journey of understanding life and the natural world. Each inspirational quote is a subjective truth—a distillation of experience and thought—meant to serve as a mirror for readers to explore their own perspectives and uncover meaning through the lens of their unique experiences.

The intention behind this book is to share a message imbued with compassion, love, and care. It is designed to inspire readers on their personal journeys and guide them toward discovering the deeper realities of life. This is not a prescriptive manual but an invitation to pause, reflect, and engage with life's profound yet simple truths.

It's important to acknowledge that neither the content nor the sequence of the quotes is intended to cause harm, discomfort, or conflict with the reader's personal beliefs. Should any part of the book feel unsettling or contradictory to one's convictions, it is purely coincidental and never intentional.

The journey through these quotes is one of openness and fluidity, free from rigid interpretations or dogmatic assertions. The content reflects the author's personal perspective, humbly offered as a source of inspiration and gentle guidance. Readers are invited to engage with the material at their own pace, to reflect deeply, and to adapt the wisdom within to align with their inner truths and life experiences.

Above all, this book aspires to spark joy, nurture connection, and encourage purposeful living. It gently beckons readers to cultivate a life rooted in compassion, integrity, and intentionality while embracing the beauty of each moment with grace and mindfulness. May the words within these pages illuminate your path as you embark on a transformative journey of self-discovery, growth, and renewal. The journey is uniquely yours, and it is an honour for the author to accompany you, even if only in spirit, as you navigate the unfolding of your life.

With this understanding, readers are encouraged to approach the book with an open mind and heart, recognising that its wisdom is offered not as universal truth but as a collection of insights shaped by the author's personal experiences. You are invited to absorb what resonates, reinterpret what feels unfamiliar, and find your own meaning within these words.

Ultimately, the author's deepest wish is that these reflections serve as a beacon of hope, a source of motivation, and a catalyst for positivity as you embark on your life-changing journey. May this book inspire you to walk your path with courage, grace, and an unwavering belief in the beauty of life's unfolding.

Note - If any part of the book, in any sequence, hurts the reader's sentiments, it would be just out of a sheer accident, not intentional

Divine

"In the tender embrace of surrender lies a profound revelation—the raw, unspoken beauty of union. Each ripple of the river becomes a whispered confession, a declaration of belonging to something greater than itself. As the river flows ceaselessly, unveiling its eternal unity with the boundless ocean, so too does the soul, in its sacred act of surrender, unveil its timeless connection to the Divine.

This surrender is not a loss but a metamorphosis of unparalleled grace, where the fragmented self dissolves into the infinite. And in that dissolution, the soul discovers the ineffable depth of its true essence—a profound oneness with the Divine, unbroken and eternal. It is a sacred symphony, an eternal melody that reverberates through the very fabric of existence, calling us back to the home we never truly left."

– Shree Shambav

EPIGRAM

"In every quiet moment lies a truth, in every tear, a teaching, and in every heartbeat, a sacred whisper. This is not just a book of quotes—it is a mirror of the soul, reflecting the beauty, fragility, and resilience of the human journey."

– Shree Shambav

Life Changing Journey

500 Inspirational Quotes

Shree Shambav

Shree Shambav is a 34x best-selling author renowned for his transformative works in personal development and spiritual growth.

Dear Cherished Readers

Dear Cherished Readers,

As I embark on this new literary voyage, my heart swells with profound gratitude and an overwhelming sense of connection. With deep emotion, I extend my heartfelt appreciation to each of you who has joined me on this journey.

With sincere warmth, I invite you to revisit the steps we have taken together through the pages of my earlier works. Our odyssey began with "Journey of Soul - Karma," a book that marked my first foray into the world of words and a testament to the raw passion that ignited my writing adventure.

The subsequent chapters of our shared narrative unfolded through the enchanting tapestry of the "Twenty + One" series. Each page turned was a brushstroke on the canvas of our imaginations, painting vivid stories that I hoped would resonate deeply within your hearts.

And how can I forget the transformative journey we embarked on with the "Life Changing Journey -

Inspirational Quotes Series." Day by day, quote by quote, we delved into reflections that uplifted, inspired, and sought to bring a glimpse of light to our souls.

The release of "Death - Light of Life and the Shadow of Death" promises to shed new light on the timeless mystery of death. Similarly, "Unleashing the Incredible Potential of Programming with Python - Optimum - PYTHON: Ultimate Guide for Beginners Series I" is poised to empower readers with newfound knowledge.

In addition, my technical book, OPTIMUM Python Series II - Exploring Data Structures and Algorithms, delves into advanced concepts in Python programming, offering a comprehensive guide for those seeking to deepen their understanding.

OPTIMUM – Python Power Series III is your essential guide to mastering the most powerful Python libraries for data science. From data manipulation and visualisation to machine learning, this book empowers you with practical tools to solve real-world challenges. Unleash your potential and transform the way you work with data.

Shree Shambav expands his artistic repertoire with "*Whispers of Eternity: 150 Plus - A Symphony of Soulful Verses*," a heartfelt exploration of the human experience. Alongside this, his "*Whispers of the Soul: A*

Journey Through Haiku" distils profound insights into poignant verses. Together, these works showcase his versatility and mastery of soulful expression, inviting readers on a journey of self-discovery. Through his poetry, he weaves a rich tapestry of emotion that resonates deeply with the heart.

Shree Shambav's latest works—*Learn to Love Yourself: A Journey of Discovering Inner Beauty and Strength Through 10 Transformative Rules, The Power of Letting Go: Embrace Freedom and Happiness, A Journey of Lasting Peace—are true treasures of self-discovery, The Entitlement Trap: Get Over It, Get On, Whispers of a Dying Soul: Unspoken Regrets and Unlived Dreams, Whispers of Silence - Unlocking Inner Power through Stillness, The Power of Words: Transforming Speech, Transforming Lives, The Art of Intentional Living: Minimalism for a Life of Purpose, Awakening the Infinite:The Power of Consciousness in Transforming Life, Beyond the Veil: A Journey Through Life After Death series, Bonds Beyond Blood - Where love builds bridges, and bonds defy blood., A Journey into Spiritual Maturity - 12 Golden Rules for Inner Transformation, The Seeker's Gold - Unlocking Life's Greatest Treasure and The Inner Battlefield - Overcoming the Enemies of the Mind and Soul.*

In addition to these works, Shree Shambav has recently ventured into astrology with the release of Astrology Unveiled – Foundations of Ancient Wisdom Series I to VIII, expanding into the realm of metaphysics. These books explore the foundational principles of Vedic astrology, offering readers a rich and practical understanding of this ancient wisdom.

Your unwavering support, enthusiasm to immerse yourself in my writings, and readiness to embark on these journeys with me have been my greatest sources of inspiration. Your input has been a beacon guiding me through the creation process, moulding these stories into containers of passion, emotion, knowledge, and resonance.

As I unveil this new narrative before you, know that your presence, insights, and shared moments have been my companions. The path we have walked together is etched in the annals of my creative evolution, and it's an honour beyond words to have you by my side once more.

Here's to the readers who have illuminated my path with their presence, who have embraced my stories with open hearts, and who have woven themselves into the very fabric of my literary world. Our journey has been a symbiotic dance of writer and reader, a harmony of souls brought together by the magic of storytelling.

With a heart brimming with appreciation and eyes glistening with anticipation, I extend my deepest gratitude for your unwavering support. Thank you for the memories, the shared emotions, and the countless hours spent in the worlds we've crafted together. As we step into this new adventure, let's continue to explore, feel, and discover the boundless horizons that words can unveil.

Warmly,

Shree Shambav

Suggested Reads

FROM BEST-SELLING AUTHOR

Endorsements

"Life-Changing Journey – Inspirational Quotes Series" is not just a collection of words—it is a soulful companion for anyone walking the path of self-discovery, healing, and transformation. Shree Shambav weaves deep wisdom with poetic grace, offering reflections that speak directly to the heart. Each page feels like a gentle whisper from the universe, reminding us of our inner strength, divine connection, and the quiet beauty of simply being human. This is a book to return to again and again—for guidance, for comfort, and for light.

- Lalitha (Advocate)

About the Author

Shree Shambav is an internationally acclaimed, best-selling author, inspirational speaker, artist, philanthropist, life coach, and entrepreneur. A world record holder, his deep passion for music led him to create soul-stirring albums, drawing inspiration from his celebrated poetry collection, Whispers of Eternity. His profound insights have sparked deep personal transformations, guiding countless individuals toward self-discovery, purposeful living, and authenticity.

With an extraordinary ability to unlock human potential, Shree empowers individuals to break through limitations and embrace their highest selves. His writings, lectures, and compassionate guidance continue to uplift lives, fostering resilience, mindfulness, and personal growth.

Shree Shambav is a 34x best-selling author celebrated for his profound contributions to personal development and spiritual growth.

Shree Shambav's literary journey took flight with the celebrated Journey of Soul - Karma, where he delved into the depths of human experience to unveil profound insights. Garnering recognition through multiple literature awards, his repertoire includes esteemed works, such as the Twenty + One Series and the enlightening Life Changing Journey series.

As a distinguished alumnus of the Indian Institute of Management and the National Institute of Technology, Shree Shambav brings a wealth of corporate acumen from his tenure in multinational corporations. His most recent publications, including Unveiling the Enigma, Death - Light of Life and the Shadow of Death and Optimum - Python Series I, Series II, and Series III demonstrate his mastery of both the literary and technical spheres.

Shree Shambav expands his artistic repertoire with "*Whispers of Eternity: 150 Plus - A Symphony of Soulful Verses*," a heartfelt exploration of the human experience. Alongside this, his "*Whispers of the Soul: A Journey Through Haiku*" distils profound insights into poignant verses. Together, these works showcase his versatility and mastery of soulful expression, inviting readers on a journey of self-discovery. Through his poetry, he weaves a rich tapestry of emotion that resonates deeply with the heart.

Shree Shambav's latest works—*Learn to Love Yourself: A Journey of Discovering Inner Beauty and Strength Through 10 Transformative Rules, The Power of Letting Go: Embrace Freedom and Happiness, A Journey of Lasting Peace—are true treasures of self-discovery, The Entitlement Trap: Get Over It, Get On, Whispers of a Dying Soul: Unspoken Regrets and Unlived Dreams, Whispers of Silence - Unlocking Inner Power through Stillness, The Power of Words: Transforming Speech, Transforming Lives, The Art of Intentional Living: Minimalism for a Life of Purpose, Awakening the Infinite:The Power of Consciousness in Transforming Life, Beyond the Veil: A Journey Through Life After Death series, Bonds Beyond Blood - Where love builds bridges, and bonds defy blood., A Journey into Spiritual Maturity - 12 Golden Rules for Inner Transformation, The Seeker's Gold - Unlocking Life's Greatest Treasure and The Inner Battlefield - Overcoming the Enemies of the Mind and Soul.*

In addition to these works, Shree Shambav has recently ventured into astrology with the release of Astrology Unveiled – Foundations of Ancient Wisdom Series I to VIII, expanding into the realm of metaphysics. These books explore the foundational principles of Vedic astrology, offering readers a rich and practical understanding of this ancient wisdom.

Shree Shambav established the Ayur Rakshita Foundation, which is dedicated to promoting boundless growth, universal fraternity, and environmental protection. The charity helps diverse communities while working for societal progress.

To learn more about Shree Shambav and his works, visit his website at www.shambav.org. For information about the Ayur Rakshita Foundation and its initiatives, visit www.shambav-ayurrakshita.org.

Let's Follow him on Social Media: **@shreeshambav**

PREFACE

Life is a symphony, where each moment plays a unique note in the grand composition of existence. Within this melody, words possess a timeless power—they awaken, heal, and inspire. *"Life Changing Journey - Inspirational Quotes Series"* by Shree Shambav is not just a collection of phrases; it is a companion, a guide, and a beacon for those navigating the intricate pathways of life.

This book was conceived in the quiet spaces where inspiration is born—in those still moments when the noise of the world fades and the soul begins to speak. Every quote in this collection distils universal truths into simple yet profound expressions, echoing the essence of human experience. Through these pages, you are invited to embark on a journey of self-discovery, reflection, and transformation.

The chapters are thoughtfully crafted, each offering a thematic exploration of the human spirit. They illuminate the courage required to embrace change, the resilience to chase dreams, and the wisdom to find meaning amid life's adversities. They delve into love and relationships, the beauty of self-acceptance, and the quiet strength that lies dormant within. These chapters whisper of joy found in simplicity, gratitude awakened through mindfulness, and the profound connection we share with the natural world and the cosmos.

This book is a tapestry woven with timeless insights that transcend circumstances. It invites you to pause, reflect, and draw inspiration from the wellspring of human wisdom. Whether you are weathering life's storms, seeking the motivation to pursue your aspirations, or yearning for the serenity of inner peace, these quotes serve as a trusted guide and confidant.

In Series III, themes like *"Embracing Change," "Discovering Self," "Dreams and Aspirations," "Embracing Imperfections," "Finding Inner Strength,"* and *"Gratitude and Mindfulness"* invite you to reflect on identity, purpose, and the pursuit of your passions.

Series IV delves deeper into *"Inspiration and Motivation," "Lessons from Adversity," "Love and Relationships," "Nature's Symphony," "Pursuing Your Dreams,"* and *"Serenity and Balance"*—nurturing connections, fostering resilience, and celebrating life's harmony.

Series V culminates in the profound, with themes like *"Shades of Existence," "Success and Achievement," "The*

Beauty of Simplicity," "The Power of Kindness," and *"Wisdom from the Ages."* These chapters remind us to cherish the beauty in life's simplest moments and draw strength from timeless truths.

Series VI culminates in a journey of inner stillness and soulful reflection, exploring themes such as *"Embracing Change," "Love and Relationships," "Serenity and Balance," "Shades of Existence," and "Whispers of the Divine."* Each chapter gently invites us to slow down, to find meaning in silence, and to recognise the sacred in everyday life. They are reminders that life's simplest moments often carry the most profound truths and that true strength arises when we listen deeply—to others, to nature, and to our hearts.

Series VII deepens this introspection, guiding us through themes like *"Discovering the Self," "Finding Inner Strength," "Lessons from Adversity," "The Power of Kindness," and "Wisdom from the Ages."* These chapters serve as lanterns on the path of growth—illuminating how hardship refines us, how kindness transforms, and how the wisdom of those who walked before us still echoes with relevance today. They remind us that every challenge holds a lesson, and every moment offers a choice to awaken.

Shree Shambav's words transcend the mundane, touching the sacred essence of life. They serve as gentle reminders of our shared humanity, encouraging us to embrace imperfections and live authentically.

Each quote is a spark—a catalyst for growth and self-discovery, illuminating the path through life's trials and triumphs.

As you turn these pages, may you find not just words but a profound connection to your inner self and the world around you. Let this collection be a sanctuary of wisdom, a reservoir of courage, and a wellspring of inspiration, empowering you to embrace life with an open heart and an awakened soul.

Welcome to the *"Life Changing Journey - Inspirational Quotes Series."* May this book inspire you to live boldly, love deeply, and discover the boundless joy within your own journey.

Let the journey unfold.

With gratitude and encouragement,

Shree Shambav

INTRODUCTION

In a world that often feels like a whirlwind of expectations, responsibilities, and endless noise, it's easy to lose sight of the deeper meaning of life. We rush through our days, chasing goals and ticking off to-do lists, yet many of us long for something more—something that grounds us, inspires us, and reconnects us to the beauty of existence.

This longing is the seed from which the *"Life Changing Journey - Inspirational Quotes Series"* was born. At its heart, this book is an invitation—a gentle call to pause, reflect, and rediscover the wisdom that lies within and around us.

Words have an extraordinary ability to shape our perspectives and transform our lives. A single phrase encountered at the right moment can shift our understanding, provide clarity in times of confusion, or ignite a spark of courage in the face of fear. This collection of quotes was curated with this transformative power in mind. Each one is a distillation of universal truths designed to speak directly to the soul and awaken the resilience, hope, and strength that reside within us all.

This book unfolds as a journey through a series of reflections, each thoughtfully curated to illuminate the many dimensions of the human experience.

Series VII deepens the journey of introspection, guiding us through transformative themes such as *"Discovering the Self," "Finding Inner Strength," "Lessons from Adversity," "The Power of Kindness," and "Wisdom from the Ages."* Each chapter becomes a lantern lighting the path of inner growth—revealing how trials become teachers, how kindness has the power to ripple through generations, and how the echoes of ancient wisdom still speak to our most modern struggles. These reflections remind us that within every hardship lies a hidden seed of strength and in every fleeting moment, a sacred opportunity to awaken, evolve, and embody the truth of who we are becoming.

Through these reflections, you will uncover the resilience to navigate life's transitions, the courage to embrace your authentic self, and the joy of living with gratitude. Each theme is a stepping stone, leading you closer to understanding the beauty of imperfection and the strength that lies within.

As you journey through these pages, you will traverse a rich tapestry of themes that reflect the multifaceted nature of life. From the courage required to embrace change to the wisdom found in adversity, the tenderness of nurturing love and relationships, and the quiet strength discovered in gratitude and simplicity—each chapter serves as a portal to deeper self-reflection and understanding.

This series is not just a collection of words but a companion for your personal growth, offering profound insights that encourage you to live authentically and harmoniously.

But this book is not meant to be read in a rush. It is not a novel to be consumed from cover to cover in one sitting. Instead, it is a companion for life's journey, offering guidance and solace whenever you need it most. You might find comfort in a quote during a moment of despair, draw courage from a phrase when facing a challenge, or uncover a fresh perspective as you navigate a crossroads.

The beauty of this collection lies in its timelessness. Whether you're at the beginning of your journey, in the midst of transformation, or reflecting on lessons learned, these quotes will meet you where you are. They are not answers but mirrors, reflecting the wisdom you already possess and encouraging you to trust your inner voice.

We live in a time where the external world demands so much of us, yet the most profound answers often come from within. This book is a reminder to listen to that quiet voice—the one that whispers truths when the world falls silent. It is a guide to help you realign with your authentic self, find purpose amidst uncertainty, and celebrate the beauty of being alive.

As you turn the pages of this book, my hope is that you discover not just inspiration but a renewed sense of connection—to yourself, to others, and to the world around you. Let these quotes be your compass, pointing you toward a life of greater meaning, joy, and fulfilment.

This journey is yours to take. With each quote, may you find the courage to embrace your unique path and the wisdom to live it fully.

Welcome to the *"Life Changing Journey - Inspirational Quotes Series."* May these words guide you toward the light within and inspire you to create a life that resonates with your truest self.

With love and gratitude,

Warm regards,

Shree Shambav

PROLOGUE

In the hush of a still moment—when the world's clamour softens and the endless doing gives way to quiet being—something sacred stirs. It is not in the towering milestones that life's deepest truths are measured but in the soft, almost imperceptible whispers of wisdom that arise in the spaces between. These whispers do not shout. They do not arrive with thunder. Instead, they emerge gently—wrapped in the ache of letting go, the warmth of shared laughter, the sting of heartbreak, and the silent strength of rising once more.

They come to us not as grand revelations but as flickers—fragments of truth carried in the wind, woven into the fabric of our everyday lives. A tear shed in solitude, a hand held in silence, a dream rekindled after despair—each becomes a sacred messenger, echoing something eternal. These moments are not just experiences; they are soul-invitations. Each one calls us to return to ourselves, to remember what we've forgotten, and to honour the quiet depth of our humanity.

This book is a collection of such whispers.

It is not a guidebook nor a prescription. It does not claim to have answers. Rather, it offers reflections—like stars scattered across a night sky—small lights that might help illuminate the terrain of your inner world. Every quote within these pages has been born from lived experience and quiet contemplation, from raw emotion and hard-won clarity. They are not written *to* you, but *for* you—for the part of you that longs to feel seen, understood, and gently awakened.

The inspiration behind this book did not arrive in a single epiphany. It came through the patient unfolding of life itself—in moments of stillness, in the quiet aftermath of grief, in the tender awe of nature, and in the sacred conversations held between the soul and the stars. The universe, it seems, speaks most clearly when we finally stop to listen.

Because life is not a linear path—it is a spiral of remembering. A mosaic of broken pieces made beautiful by the light that shines through the cracks. It is a dance between chaos and grace, between pain and peace, between losing ourselves and finding something far deeper than we imagined.

This book is an invitation to pause. To breathe. To return.

To that space within you that holds your truest knowing—the one that survives the noise, the expectations, and the fears. It is for the dreamers who yearn for something more, the seekers who walk through shadow in search of light, and the quiet warriors who carry their questions like sacred flames.

As you turn these pages, may you find echoes of your own story—the parts that hurt, the parts that healed, and the parts still becoming. These words are not tied to any one voice or journey. They are a chorus of our shared humanity. They remind us that even when we feel most alone, we are part of something vast, interconnected, and divinely unfolding.

This is not just a book—it is a companion for the soul. A flicker of warmth in moments of cold. A hand extended through the pages. A mirror reflecting back the beauty, resilience, and radiant truth that already lives inside you.

Welcome to *The Life-Changing Journey – Inspirational Quotes Series.*

With reverence, with hope, and with love,
– Shree Shambav

.

CONTENTS

Discovering Self

Reflections on Identity and Purpose

"You are not what the world sees, but what your soul remembers when everything else is silent. In the stillness, your true self emerges—not as an image, but as an essence."

- *Shree Shambav*

Awareness

The Lightbearer: Awareness is the compass that points us to the light within; with it, even the darkest battles transform into lessons, and every defeat becomes a step toward liberation.

Chains of Love

"Sometimes, love isn't the freedom to soar; it's the weight of chains we choose to carry, hoping they'll someday loosen into wings."

Echoes of Endurance

"Resilience is not the absence of pain but the quiet resolve to stand amidst the ruins, waiting for the light to find its way back."

Grace in Goodbye

"Sometimes, the greatest strength is found in the quiet grace of saying goodbye to what you love most."

Hope Between the Cracks

"Even in the crumbling walls of a fractured bond, a single bloom of hope can find its way through, reminding us that not all is lost."

On Destiny and Detours

"Not all who wander are lost, but some who stay still never find their way home."

On Finding Home

"Home is not always a place—it is sometimes a person, a memory, or the way the stars align when we feel at peace."

On the Music of Longing

"Not all music is heard with the ears—some songs live in the rhythm of a heartbeat, in the hush of a longing that refuses to fade."

On the Power of Letting Go

"To let go is not to forget, but to set the heart free from carrying what was never meant to be caged."

On the Shadows of the Past

"The past never truly leaves us—it merely waits in quiet corners, woven into the echoes of who we are becoming."

On the Sound of Goodbye

"Every goodbye has an aftersound—a silent echo that lingers, waiting to be heard in the quietest moments of the soul."

Resilience Beyond Survival

"Resilience is not just enduring the storm but learning to dance in its rain, finding beauty in the struggle, and forging strength from every tear."

Rising from the Shadows

"The weight of your past does not anchor you; it teaches you to rise. Every scar, every fall, is but a stepping stone toward your highest self."

Roots That Hold

"Strength isn't in the absence of storms but in the roots that hold you steady when they rage."

Roots and Wings

"The deeper your roots, the higher you can soar, for the strongest trees embrace both the earth below and the sky above."

Roots and Wings

"The strongest trees are those whose roots run deep and whose branches reach wide. Balance lies in knowing when to stay grounded and when to let the wind carry you higher."

Roots of Guilt

"Guilt is not a punishment; it's a shadow. It follows you, reminding you not of what you did, but of what you didn't."

Shadows of Unspoken Words

"The loudest silences are the ones between two hearts that once spoke in whispers but now echo with words left unsaid."

Shattered Reflections

"When the cracks in a dream begin to show, they do not merely break the illusion—they reveal the truths we've long been afraid to face."

Stars and Choices

"Destiny may script the stars, but it's our choices that write the soul's story."

Strength in Silence

"Not all battles are fought with swords; some are fought in silence, with clenched fists and whispered prayers, where survival itself is the victory."

The Alchemy of Forgiveness

"Forgiveness does not erase the past—it transforms it, turning the weight of pain into the wings of freedom."

The Alchemy of Resilience

"True strength is not found in the absence of struggle but in the quiet resilience that turns pain into wisdom and fear into courage."

The Architect of Fate

"You are not merely a traveller on this journey of life—you are the architect of your own destiny, sculpting beauty from chaos and light from darkness."

The Art of Detachment

"Detachment is not indifference; it is the ability to hold the world lightly, without letting it weigh down the spirit."

The Art of Holding Lightly

"Detachment is not about turning away from life but learning to hold it gently, like water cupped in your hands—free to flow, free to nourish."

The Art of Letting Go

"A river does not mourn the mountains it leaves behind, nor does the sky cling to the clouds that pass. To love deeply is to hold with open hands and to let go without fear."

The Cost of Love

"To love deeply is to surrender a part of yourself—not as a loss, but as a gift. Love is not about possession; it is about the willingness to give, even when it is painful."

The Courage to Rise

"Failure is not the end, but the teacher. Each fall is an invitation to rise stronger, with wisdom etched into our very being."

The Dance of Impermanence

"Life's beauty lies in its impermanence. Like a flame flickering in the wind, its fragility reminds us to cherish each moment."

The Depth of Purpose

"Purpose is the bridge between fleeting desires and lasting fulfilment. When we align with it, every step becomes sacred."

The Echo of Choices

"A man's life is not defined by the roads he takes, but by the ones he walks away from and the echoes of the choices he cannot undo."

The Echo of Unspoken Words

"Regret is not born from the choices we make, but from the words we never say, the love we never express, and the moments we let slip away while waiting for the 'right time.'"

The Echoes of Betrayal

"A blade in the back is not always held by an enemy. Sometimes, it is placed by a friend who simply chooses himself over you."

The Fire Within

"Greatness is not given, nor is it found—it is forged in the fire of struggle, tempered by wisdom, and carried by those who dare to believe in the unseen."

The Fire Within

"The world will try to tame the fire in your soul—dousing it with doubt, burying it beneath expectations. But those who change destiny are the ones who refuse to let their flames die."

The Fragility of Love

"Love doesn't break like glass—it erodes like stone in a river, slowly, silently, until all that remains is a shape you no longer recognise."

The Freedom of Letting Go

"In clinging to outcomes, we become prisoners of our fears. But in releasing our grip, we find the courage to live fully, without the chains of expectation."

The Garden of Fulfilment

"Life blooms most beautifully when we become gardeners of detachment—nurturing what we have with care but allowing each flower to blossom and fade in its own time."

The Gift of Humility

"Greatness is not in reaching the summit but in remembering the hands that held you steady on the climb."

The Heart of Leadership

"Leadership is not the weight of power on your shoulders; it is the light of your heart guiding others through their darkest moments."

The Illusion of Control

"Strategy can shape a battle, but it cannot command the hearts of men. The greatest victories are won not with the sword, but with trust."

The Illusion of Control

"The tighter we grip the reins of life, the more we lose sight of its natural flow. True strength lies in surrender, not in control."

The Illusion of Having It All

"You can chase the world and call it ambition, or you can embrace love and call it home. But know this—if you spend too long chasing, you may return to find that home no longer waits for you."

The Illusion of Possession

"We spend our lives chasing what we think we lack, only to realise that the greatest treasures were never meant to be owned—only understood."

The Illusion of Time

"We chase dreams as if time is infinite, only to wake up one day and realise that the greatest treasure was the moments we let slip away."

The Illusion of Time

"We live as if we have forever, yet time slips through our fingers like sand. The question is not how much time we have, but what we choose to do with the moments given to us."

The Journey Home

"We search the world for riches, only to return and find that the greatest treasure was never hidden—it was always within us, waiting to be discovered."

The Journey and the Destination

"A traveller who fears the road will never know the beauty of distant lands. Walk forward—not because the path is clear, but because your soul was never meant to stand still."

The Journey or the Destination

"Some chase the horizon, believing fulfilment lies beyond the next mountain. Others walk with eyes open, realising that every step taken in awareness is the destination itself."

The Lens of the Soul

"The world does not change; it is the eyes that behold it that transform reality into either a prison or a paradise."

The Light Beyond Darkness

"Even in the deepest shadows, a spark of light remains. Seek it, nurture it, and let it guide you home."

The Meaning of True Legacy

"Gold can buy you a name, but only wisdom can make it last beyond your final breath. A man is not remembered for what he owned, but for what he gave."

The Measure of Legacy

"True legacy is not written in wealth or power, but in the hearts we touch, the love we give, and the wisdom we leave behind."

The Merging of Destinies

"Marriage is not the end of one's journey, but the birth of a shared path. It is not about losing oneself, but about growing into something greater—together."

The Mirror Within

"Every anger we hold, every fear we hide, is a reflection of the battle within. Heal the mirror, and the world becomes clearer."

The Paradox of Strength

"Strength is not in how much we can carry, but in what we are willing to set down. True power is not in control, but in surrendering to the wisdom of the unknown."

The Path of Purpose

"When life feels heavy and directionless, remember: purpose is not found in the world outside but in the steady flame of meaning within your heart."

The Path to Inner Freedom

"Freedom is not found in the absence of obstacles but in the presence of unwavering self-awareness amidst them."

The Power of Inner Stillness

"In the quiet spaces of the heart, where the noise of the world fades, the soul whispers truths that words cannot express."

The Power of Presence

"To live fully is not to chase every fleeting desire but to meet each moment with the undivided attention of the soul."

The Price of Ambition

"A man who chases the world may one day hold it in his hands, but what use is a kingdom if his soul is lost along the way?"

The Price of Growth

"The cost of becoming who you are meant to be is often the comfort of who you used to be. The question is—are you willing to pay the price?"

The Quiet Strength of Forgiveness

"Forgiveness is not the acceptance of wrong but the liberation of the soul from chains it was never meant to wear."

The Silent Language of Love

"Love is not measured in words spoken, but in burdens shared, in sacrifices made, and in the quiet understanding between two souls who choose each other every day."

The Strength in Vulnerability

"To be strong is not to stand tall in silence but to kneel in honesty and say, 'I cannot carry this alone.'"

The Tapestry of Life and Time

"Life, with its intricate tapestry of experiences, gently guides us to use time wisely, to cherish the now. Yet, it is time, relentless and unyielding, that ultimately teaches us the true worth of life, urging us to live fully, to love deeply, and to leave no word unspoken."

The Weight of Choices

"A single decision is like a pebble dropped in a pond; its ripples may be small at first, but they stretch far beyond what the eye can see. Choose not just with your mind, but with the wisdom of your heart."

The Weight of Doubt

"Doubt is a heavy chain, forged in fear, that keeps the heart from seeing the light in others. But trust—trust is the key that sets it free."

The Weight of Dreams

"A dream is not a feather that drifts aimlessly in the wind—it is a stone carried in the heart. It will either anchor you in fear or become the foundation upon which you build your destiny."

The Weight of Love

"Love is not a chain, nor is it freedom—it is the space between, where two souls meet not to possess, but to belong."

The Weight of Power

"Power is not a throne one sits upon, but a storm one learns to stand within. The moment you believe you control it, it begins to control you."

The Weight of Sacrifice

"True sacrifice is not measured by what we lose but by what we preserve—our love, our hope, and the souls of those who depend on us."

The Weight of Silence

"Not all prisons have walls, and not all chains are made of iron. Some are woven from silence—the words we never speak, the truths we never face, the dreams we leave unchased."

The Weight of Silence

"Silence is not emptiness; it is a storm held within, a battle fought without the luxury of being heard."

The Weight of Silence

"The heaviest burden is not the one we carry in our arms but the one we bury in our hearts—unsaid, unseen, and slowly breaking us from within."

The Weight of Silent Love

"Love isn't about claiming someone; it's about giving them the freedom to find their happiness, even if it leaves you empty."

The Weight of True Freedom

"Freedom is not the absence of commitment, but the presence of a purpose worth dedicating oneself to. Without direction, even the open sky can feel like a cage."

The Whisper of Hope

"Hope is the whisper that reminds us, even in our darkest hour, that dawn is just on the horizon."

The Whisper of Potential

"In the silence of self-discovery, we find the whispers of our true potential waiting to be heard."

The Wisdom of Stillness

"In the stillness of your heart, you will find the answers you seek. Silence is not emptiness; it is the space where wisdom is born."

The Wisdom of Surrender

"Surrender is not defeat; it is the recognition that there is something greater than your individual will at work. Surrender brings peace, and peace brings clarity."

The Wisdom of the Journey

"The journey is as important as the destination. Every struggle, every triumph, is part of the story that shapes who you are becoming."

Threads of Destiny

"In the tapestry of life, our habits are the threads that bind our fate, stitching together the story of who we are and who we strive to become."

Threads of Fidelity

"In the tapestry of morality, cheating paints the hues of choice, staining relationships with the brush of deception. Meanwhile, loyalty emerges as the masterpiece of responsibility, woven with threads of commitment and unwavering fidelity."

Triumph Shared, Triumph Multiplied

"Victory that uplifts only the victor is hollow. True triumph is when your success becomes the seed of hope and opportunity for those around you."

True Beauty

"We remove the masks and reveal the true beauty of who we are when we confront ourselves with unwavering honesty, opening the door to a life filled with love and authenticity."

True Empathy

"True empathy is not merely a feeling for others but seeing through their eyes, understanding their reality, and respecting their journey as valid as your own."

Trust Over Tales

"The allure of exaggeration fades, but the strength of truth builds trust that endures."

Trusting Strengths

"To teach a fish to swim is to trust in its ability to navigate the waters, just as we must trust in others' unique strengths."

Trusting the Rhythm of Your Path

"Your journey is a story that only you can tell. Trust in its rhythm, and know that every step, even the uncertain ones, leads you closer to the life meant for you."

Two Faces, One Soul

"To the world, she wore a smile painted with lies, but in the quiet of her solitude, she pieced together her truth, one fragment at a time."

Uniqueness in Vision

"While we may possess a common gift of two eyes, the vistas they unveil are uniquely ours. The world unfolds through the lens of individual views, reminding us that in the grand gallery of existence, diversity of perspectives is the brushstroke that adds depth and richness to our collective portrait."

Unlocking Inner Beauty

"Self-love is the key to unlocking the profound beauty within, allowing us to see our true worth and radiate it outward."

Unseen Depths

"What lies before us may test our limits, but it is the unseen depths of our soul that harbour the true essence of our potential and courage."

Unspoken Connections

"The deepest connections are formed not in words spoken, but in the unspoken understanding of shared souls."

Veil of Desire

"Like a veil over a flame, desire cloaks the brilliance of one's knowledge, casting shadows upon the clarity of understanding. Only through the gentle breeze of introspection can the smoke dissipate, revealing the radiant truth within."

Vessels of Change

"As we navigate the currents of self-development, we become vessels of change, vessels whose every stride towards progress sets in motion a ripple effect of growth in the lives of others. In our ascent, we carry the collective hopes of humanity, forging a path where personal evolution intertwines with the advancement of the world."

Whispers of Stories

"The vast realm of imagination waiting to be discovered lies in the silent whispers of stories, between the lines and beneath the words."

Wisdom's Crucible

"In the crucible of life's challenges, true wisdom emerges, transforming the ordinary into the extraordinary."

Finding Inner Strength

Empowering the Mind and Spirit

"You are not defined by what breaks you, but by the stillness that remains when everything else has fallen away. That is your unshakable core—untouched, eternal."

- *Shree Shambav*

A Space for Growth

"Clearing physical clutter is not just an act of tidying up; it's a declaration of self-respect—a commitment to create a space where your mind can breathe, your heart can focus, and your soul can thrive."

Between Two Suns

"Ambition is a sun that blinds; love is a sun that warms. Walk too far in either direction, and you will either burn or freeze."

Beyond the Horizon

"The mind seeks answers in the world, but meditation unveils the boundless universe within."

Beyond the Veil of Fear

"Fear is not a wall but a shadow—intimidating until you walk through it. The truth is not hidden; it is only veiled by the illusions we cling to."

Clearing Clutter, Finding Stillness

"When we clear the clutter from our homes, we create space to quiet the chaos within. In that stillness, we find clarity, focus, and a deeper connection to what truly matters."

Clouds and Sky

"Thoughts are fleeting clouds, but consciousness is the sky that holds them. Meditation connects you to the sky."

Creating Space for Joy

"Minimalism isn't about having less; it's about creating space for more of what truly matters—more joy, more connection, and more of the things that align with your deepest purpose."

Deathless Awareness

"To mature is to awaken to the truth that while the body perishes, the soul dances eternally beyond time's grasp."

Discovering the Loudest Truths

"In the quiet spaces created by minimalism, we find the loudest truths of the soul—clarity, connection, and the freedom to truly discover who we are."

Freedom from the Transient

"Maturity is the liberation from clinging to what fades, and the embrace of what eternally abides."

Gratitude, the Alchemist of the Heart

"Gratitude turns jealousy into joy, scarcity into abundance, and resentment into reverence. When you bless what you admire, you invite the same grace into your life."

Inner Treasure

"Wealth fades, fame withers, but the treasure of meditation enriches the soul forever."

Love Without Chains

"To love something is to let it be free. To chain it is to love not the thing itself, but our fear of losing it."

Love and Attachment

"Love whispers, 'I cherish you as you are.' Attachment demands, 'Be what I need you to be.' One sets free, the other binds."

Making Space for Transformation

"In the act of letting go, we make room not just for new things, but for new ways of being—where clarity, purpose, and peace can finally take root."

Nature's Reflection

"In the quiet embrace of nature, we find a mirror to our soul—each leaf, each breeze, gently reminding us of the peace that resides within, waiting to be uncovered."

Purposeful Minimalism

"Minimalism is not the absence of things, but the presence of purpose. It is the deliberate clearing of distractions, creating space for the clarity and focus on what truly nourishes our soul and aligns with our deepest values."

Ripples of Intentional Living

"When you live with intention and simplicity, your life becomes a beacon, inspiring others to let go of excess and embrace what truly matters—creating ripples of change that extend to the world around you."

Room for What Matters

"Minimalism isn't about having less; it's about making room for more of what matters."

Silent Awakening

"True growth begins when the noise of the mind is replaced by the stillness of awareness."

The Art of Letting Go

"Detachment is not the absence of love but the presence of wisdom. It is knowing that love does not require ownership to be real."

The Awakening Soul

"Maturity is the soul's awakening from the dream of mortality into the reality of eternal being."

The Beauty in Imperfection

"Just as a cracked pot spills water to nourish the flowers along the path, our imperfections can become the very source of beauty that enriches the lives we touch."

The Beauty of Letting Go

"What is meant to stay will stay without force, and what is meant to leave will leave despite our grasp. In letting go, we welcome life as it is, not as we wish it to be."

The Burden of Regret

"Regret is a shadow that follows you, always lurking, never letting you escape what you've lost in the pursuit of what you thought you wanted."

The Cage of Endless Desires

"A man who seeks everything will find nothing, for his hands will always be too full to hold what truly matters."

The Chains of Clinging

"That which you hold onto most tightly is what holds you captive. Release your grip, and you will find that freedom was never outside—it was always within."

The Container and the Contents

"The mind obsesses over the contents of life, but meditation reveals the infinite container holding it all."

The Cost of Abandonment

"We are taught to chase our dreams, but what are we left with when those dreams demand the abandonment of the ones we love?"

The Cost of True Friendship

"True friendship is not measured by what you can give, but by what you've given when you had nothing to offer."

The Empty Vessel

"A cup that is full can hold no more. A mind filled with pride leaves no space for wisdom to enter."

The Essence of Choice

"The meaning of minimalism lies not in what we remove, but in what we choose to keep."

The Eternal Sky

"Meditation is not about chasing the clouds of thought but discovering the infinite sky of your inner being."

The Fire That Consumes

"Jealousy is like fire—it does not warm you; it burns you. And the more you feed it, the more it consumes, until nothing remains but ashes of the self you once were."

The Fire Within

"Envy burns like wildfire, consuming the heart that harbours it. But a soul kindled with gratitude and inspiration transforms its flames into light, warming the world instead of scorching it."

The Fragility of Power

"Palaces of ambition crumble like castles of sand, but the foundation of self-awareness stands eternal."

The Freedom of Letting Go

"When we let go of what no longer serves us, we create space not just for new things, but for new possibilities—the freedom to live intentionally, aligned with our deepest values and dreams."

The Game of Life

"Life becomes meaningful not by the games we win but by the depths of silence we discover within."

The Gift of Gratitude

"Gratitude is the antidote to jealousy. When you truly see what is already yours, the desire for what belongs to another fades like mist before the morning sun."

The Gift of Reconnection

"Sometimes, the greatest gift we can give ourselves is the freedom to return to what we once thought we had outgrown."

The Hands of a Closed Fist

"A jealous heart is like a clenched fist—it cannot hold love, it cannot receive grace, and it cannot offer kindness. Only when the hand opens can it truly grasp life's abundance."

The Heart of Ambition

"Ambition is a fire that burns bright, but without balance, it consumes all that it touches."

The Heart's Longing

"A man can cross the world in search of treasure, but it's the journey back to his heart that holds the true wealth."

The Hollow Crown

"Power and wealth may build empires, but they cannot fill the void left by a restless heart."

The Hunger for Validation

"A heart that craves validation will never be full. The more it feeds on praise, the emptier it becomes."

The Illusion of Abundance

"A man may own the world, yet if his soul is barren, he will still feel poor."

The Illusion of Competition

"A flower does not compare itself to another; it simply blooms. The ocean does not envy the sky; it simply exists in its vastness. Let go of competition, and you will know peace."

The Illusion of Life

"What we call life is but a shadow of true living; only in meditation do we find the light."

The Illusion of Loss

"We often search for what was never lost, only hidden in the corners of our hearts, waiting to be remembered."

The Illusion of Ownership

"Not even the body you call your own belongs to you; it is borrowed from the earth, destined to return."

The Illusion of Possession

"Nothing in this world is truly owned—neither people, nor time, nor even the body that houses you. To accept this is to find peace."

The Illusion of Possession

"Nothing truly belongs to us—not people, not wealth, not even time. The tighter we grasp, the more life slips through our fingers. Only in letting go do we finally hold the infinite."

The Illusion of Possession

"You claim ownership over people, things, even time itself. But in truth, nothing belongs to you—not even your own breath. To understand this is to taste liberation."

The Illusion of Superiority

"Pride whispers that you are above others; wisdom reminds you that all are made of dust and to dust shall return."

The Impermanence of All Things

"Like footprints on the shore, all things fade with time. Clinging to the tide will not keep it from retreating—only by flowing with it does one remain at peace."

The Liberation of Letting Go

"To let go of pride is to remove the weight that binds the soul. The lightest step is taken by the one who carries nothing but wisdom."

The Liberation of Minimalism

"The true depth of minimalism is not found in the simplicity of our surroundings, but in the liberation, centeredness it brings to our hearts—an invitation to reconnect with what truly nourishes our soul and live with a clarity that rises above the chaos of the world."

The Liberation of the Soul

"The moment you stop wishing for another's life and start embracing your own, jealousy dies, and peace is born. True freedom begins where envy ends."

The Light That Awakens

"You do not find truth—you remember it. Like the sun behind the clouds, it was never gone, only waiting for the winds of awareness to clear the sky."

The Light Within

"True fulfilment is not found in riches or power but in the love, purpose, and wisdom we nurture within."

The Light of Self-Acceptance

"When we learn to love our imperfections, we open the door to self-discovery, allowing the light of acceptance to illuminate the path toward inner serenity."

The Mirage of Possession

"Envy is the illusion that what belongs to another was meant for us. But the river does not envy the rain, nor does the mountain envy the sky—each exists in its own fullness."

The Mirror of Meditation

"Meditation reflects not who you think you are, but the eternal essence of who you truly are."

The Mirror of Self-Doubt

"What we envy in others is often what we fear we lack within ourselves. If their light makes us feel small, it is not because they shine too brightly—it is because we have forgotten to kindle our flame."

The Mirror of Truth

"Pride is a mirror that reflects only what we want to see. Humility is the hand that wipes it clean, revealing the truth beyond our illusions."

The Mirror of the Mind

"Comparison is the mirror that distorts your reflection—look too long into another's life, and you forget the beauty of your own."

The Nature of Faith and Fate

"Fate may chart our course, but faith is what gives us the strength to choose our own path."

The Open Hand of Wisdom

"The clenched fist of arrogance holds onto illusion, while the open hand of humility receives truth."

The Peace of Acceptance

"True peace is not the absence of flaws but the acceptance of our human experience; it is in our imperfections that we learn compassion and grace."

The Price of Trust

"Betrayal doesn't just shatter trust—it dissects the very fabric of who we are, leaving us to pick up the pieces of our identity."

The Prison of Comparison

"Jealousy is not the thief of joy—comparison is. When we measure our worth against another, we lock ourselves in a prison of discontent, blind to the abundance already within us."

The Reflection of Lack

"Jealousy is not born from another's success but from our own sense of lack. The wise do not resent the sunrise in another's life; they turn inward and ignite their own dawn."

The Regret That Comes Too Late

"The greatest sorrow is not losing a parent, but realising too late that you never truly cherished them while they were still there."

The Return to Self

"In the search for the world, we lose ourselves; in returning to ourselves, we find everything we ever needed."

The Richness in Stillness

"In the stillness of less, we discover the richness of what truly matters—because it is only when we let go of the noise that we can hear the quiet call of our deepest purpose."

The River's Wisdom

"A river never mourns the water that has passed, nor does it fear the water that is yet to come. It flows, knowing change is its nature."

The Shadow of Ego

"A proud man walks under the sun, thinking his shadow makes him taller. But it is only an illusion cast by the light of his own ignorance."

The Shadow of Envy

"A jealous heart does not see what it lacks; it only sees what another has. But shadows exist only where light is blocked—remove the envy, and your own light will shine."

The Silence of the Ocean

"The shallow stream makes noise about its greatness, but the deepest ocean holds its power in silence. True wisdom flows in quiet humility."

The Silent Destroyer

"Pride does not announce its arrival; it creeps in like a shadow, whispering that you are above others. Only self-awareness can dissolve its hold."

The Silent Killer of Love

"Envy and love cannot live in the same heart. One seeks to elevate, the other to diminish. One rejoices in abundance, the other suffers in scarcity. Choose love, and jealousy will wither."

The Strength of Humility

"Humility is not thinking less of yourself; it is thinking beyond yourself. It is the wisdom of knowing that no wave is greater than the ocean it belongs to."

The Strength of the Bowing Tree

"A tree that stands rigid in a storm will break, but the one that bows will endure. Humility is not surrender; it is survival."

The Treasure of Vulnerability

"Embracing our flaws is like discovering hidden treasures; in our vulnerabilities, we find the raw authenticity that connects us to ourselves and others."

The True Battlefield"

"The greatest battles are not fought with swords or words, but within the silent chambers of the soul. To conquer the world is fleeting, but to conquer oneself is eternal victory."

The Turn Inward

"To journey outward is to chase illusions; to journey inward is to encounter reality."

The Veil of Illusion

"Pride is the fog that clouds the mirror of truth. The more you cling to the image of yourself, the less you see who you truly are."

The Veil of Pride

"Pride is a veil woven from illusions—it blinds the eyes, deafens the ears, and silences the soul. Only humility can lift it and reveal the truth beneath."

The Weight of Clinging

"What we hold too tightly begins to own us, and in our fear of losing, we forget how to truly live."

The Weight of Holding On

"That which is clutched too tightly turns to dust. The tighter the grip, the deeper the pain when it slips away."

The Weight of Possession

"That which you cling to most tightly will be the first to slip from your grasp. True freedom is found in open hands, not clenched fists."

The Weight of Power

"Power does not make you free; it makes you a prisoner to the expectations of others."

The Weight of Silence

"True understanding is born not in speech, but in silence. When the noise of the mind settles, wisdom rises like the first light of dawn—gentle, yet all-encompassing."

The Weight of Silent Prayers

"Sometimes the prayers we whisper into the silence are the ones that shape us the most."

The Weight of Unspoken Goodbyes

"Some roads take us forward, but at the cost of what we leave behind. The question is—was the journey worth the silence of those we once loved?"

The Weight of the Empty Throne

"The higher one climbs the mountain of pride, the lonelier the peak becomes. True kingship is not in ruling others but in mastering oneself."

The Whisper of Peace

"When we walk among the trees and listen to the whispers of the wind, we reconnect with the stillness that transcends all chaos, discovering that peace is not something we seek, but something we remember."

The Wisdom of Detachment

"To walk lightly upon this earth, one must hold everything with open hands, ready to receive, ready to release, never clinging, never fearing."

Timelessness Within

"Meditation is not an escape from life but a return to the timeless core of existence."

Uncovering Your True Life

"Minimalism is not about what you remove; it's about what you uncover—a life centred on your deepest values, free from the noise that once held you back."

Lessons from Adversity

Turning Challenges into Growth

Adversity does not arrive to break you—it arrives to reveal you. Like fire purifies gold, challenges strip away the surface to uncover the brilliance beneath."

- *Shree Shambav*

Adversity

Life's Sculptor: "Adversity is the chiselling force of life, shaping the raw stone of our being into the masterpiece of who we are meant to become."

Breaking Invisible Chains

"The true prison we face is not the world around us, but the constant whisper of fear that others' perceptions can control the direction of our lives."

Climbing Beyond Limitation

"What we truly need is not mercy to soften our fall, but opportunity to climb higher. It is through the doors of opportunity that we escape the shackles of limitation and find the freedom to become who we were always meant to be."

Courage Over Obstacles

"Dreams are not bound by the weight of obstacles, but are fuelled by the courage to rise above them. Each step forward, no matter how small, is a victory over doubt and fear."

Embracing the Storm

"Life is an ocean with waves that may never rest; peace is found not in waiting for calm waters, but in learning the grace of swimming through the storm."

Empowerment Through Adversity

"Mercy is a balm for the broken, but it is an opportunity that empowers us to rise. We don't seek to be spared from our struggles; we seek the path to overcome them, knowing that within every chance lies the seed of greatness."

Flowing with the Universe

"To flow with the universe is not to abandon yourself but to find yourself in every wave of its unfolding."

Freedom with Purpose

"True freedom is not the absence of boundaries, but the presence of purpose."

Growth Amidst Life's Storms

"The truest growth is not measured by what we achieve, but by how deeply we learn to listen to the whispers of our soul amidst life's storms."

Growth Through Honesty

"In the face of deceit, let not bitterness take root. Embrace the clarity that truth brings, for it is only through honesty that we truly grow."

Letting Go of Control

"When we let go of the need to control, we make space for the universe to reveal its perfect plan."

Ripples of Love

"Every step you take on the path of love ripples through eternity."

Strength Born of Struggle

"Adversity is not the end of the road, but the beginning of transformation. In every struggle lies a lesson, and in every lesson, the seed of a strength you never knew you possessed."

Strength in Stillness

"In the stillness of each breath, we find the quiet strength that leads us back to our centre, reminding us that peace is already within."

Strength in Vulnerability

"In the shades of existence, we discover the true radiance of life—where every moment of darkness reveals the depth of our light. It is in our vulnerabilities that we find our strength, and in the quiet, we awaken to our true essence."

Success in Every Step

"Success is not the destination, but the unfolding of your potential in every step you take. Achievement is born from the courage to push past your limits, to rise again after every fall, and to trust in the power of your own growth."

The Alchemy of Courage

"Fear and courage are born from the same seed. One withers in doubt; the other blossoms in faith. Choose which one you water, and it will shape your destiny."

The Alchemy of Pain

"Pain is not the end of us, but the fire that forges us. It turns longing into wisdom, sorrow into depth, and loss into a love that never fades."

The Art of Becoming

"To carry guilt forever is to chain yourself to a moment that no longer exists. True growth comes when you forgive yourself enough to become who you were meant to be."

The Art of Letting Go

"Some things slip from our grasp, not because we are weak, but because they were never meant to be held. Letting go is not loss—it is wisdom."

The Art of Letting Go

"What you cling to owns you. Only by letting go do you truly hold freedom in your hands."

The Art of Stillness

"A storm may rage, but the mountain does not chase the wind. Strength is not in endless movement, but in the power to stand unmoved in chaos."

The Battle Within

"Conquering the world is easy compared to conquering the restless mind. For the true battlefield is not outside, but within."

The Beginning of Freedom

"Freedom begins when we stop seeking approval from others and start embracing the truth of who we are, unafraid of the opinions that try to bind us."

The Cage of Expectation

"We suffer not because life is unkind, but because we demand it to be otherwise. Happiness is not in control, but in surrendering to what is."

The Canvas of Darkness

"Darkness is not the absence of light but the canvas upon which the stars write their eternal stories."

The Catalyst of Transformation

"Mercy may soothe the wounds of the past, but it is an opportunity that ignites the fire of transformation. In the space where chance meets preparation, we discover our true potential, not in the pity of others, but in the possibilities we seize."

The Chains of Comfort

"We do not fear change—we fear losing who we were. But the caterpillar does not resist the cocoon, nor the seed refuse the soil. Growth is not the death of self, but the becoming of what was always meant to be."

The Courage to Break

"A heart that has never broken has never truly lived. It is in the breaking that we learn to mend, in the shattering that we learn to shine."

The Dance of Dreams and Courage

"Inspiration whispers to the soul, awakening dreams buried beneath the weight of life. Motivation takes those dreams by the hand, guiding them into the light, where courage turns possibility into reality."

The Dance of Life

"Life is not about chasing what you desire, but about flowing with the rhythm of existence, surrendering to its mysteries without resistance."

The Depth of Presence

"To be fully present is to taste eternity in a single moment."

The Discovery in Surrender

"In surrender, you do not lose yourself; you discover the infinite within you."

The Echo of Fear

"Fear whispers of dangers unseen, shadows unproven, and endings that never come. The wise do not silence fear—they listen, understand, and walk forward anyway."

The Embrace of the Soul

"The soul's journey is not in escaping the world, but in embracing it with open arms and an open heart."

The Essence of Balance

"Inner peace blooms when we release the need to control and embrace the flow of life. In the stillness of acceptance, we discover the true essence of balance."

The Eternal Journey

"The journey is never about reaching the destination; it is about becoming the one who can walk the path without fear."

The Fire Within

"A candle does not lose its flame by lighting another. Share your light freely, for it is in giving that the soul burns brightest."

The Fire Within

"A candle does not mourn the darkness; it simply burns. Fear waits for the night to end—courage becomes the light that ends it."

The Fire of Transformation

"A life untouched by struggle is like unburned incense—full of fragrance but never releasing its true essence."

The Heart's Silent Language

"The heart whispers truths the mind cannot comprehend; silence is its only language."

The Illusion of Control

"A man grips the sand tighter, thinking he will hold onto more, but the tighter he clenches, the faster it slips away. Control is not in grasping, but in surrendering."

The Illusion of Control

"The leaf does not resist the wind, yet it travels farther than the stone that clings to the ground."

The Illusion of Time

"We grieve for the past, fear for the future, and forget that both exist only in the mind. True peace is found in the depth of this moment."

The Journey as the Achievement

"True success is found not in the accolades we collect, but in the quiet strength we build within, the resilience to rise after each setback, and the unwavering belief that our journey is the most profound achievement of all."

The Joy of Being

"True joy does not come from what we acquire or achieve, but from the simple act of being—being present, being aware, and being alive."

The Leap Beyond Fear

"A bird does not test each gust of wind before it flies. It leaps, trusting its wings and the sky. Let your faith be the wind beneath your doubt."

The Light Within

"Do not seek the light outside; it has always been within you, waiting for your eyes to open."

The Light Within

"The light you seek in the world is the same light that burns quietly within your soul."

The Mind's Prison

"Fear is not the walls around you but the ones within. You do not escape fear by running from it—you dissolve it by stepping beyond its illusion."

The Mirror of Truth

"To see oneself as one truly is—to stand before the mirror of truth without fear—is the first step toward liberation."

The Mirror of the Soul

"We seek love in another's eyes, wisdom in another's words, and strength in another's presence. But the mirror we avoid holds all we search for."

The Mirror of the Soul

"You do not see the world as it is; you see it as you are. To change your reality, first cleanse the mirror of your soul."

The Path and the Traveller

"The road does not ask the traveller where he is going; it only stretches before him. It is not the certainty of the destination, but the courage to walk that shapes the journey."

The Path of Wonder

"The path to truth is not walked with the feet but with a heart open to wonder."

The Path of the Seeker

"The true seeker does not chase the truth like a prize but walks with it like an old friend, knowing it was never lost."

The Poetry of Presence

"To truly love is not to promise forever, but to be fully present in the moment. Love is not a vow—it is a presence, a poetry written in the now."

The Prison of Fear

"The most confining prison is not made of walls, but of the invisible chains forged by our fear of others' judgments, keeping us captive in a life, not our own."

The Prison of Guilt

"Guilt is a heavy door locked from the inside. Forgiveness is not waiting on the other side—it is the key in your own hand."

The Prison of Illusion

"Ignorance is not darkness—it is the refusal to open our eyes. The blind man does not suffer from blindness, but from his unwillingness to learn a new way to see."

The Quiet Voice of the Divine

"The divine does not speak in grand gestures, but in the quiet moments between heartbeats."

The Radiance of Shadows

"The light of life shines brightest not in the absence of shadows but in the way we embrace them. Each shade reveals a hidden truth, and in the interplay of light and dark, we find the full spectrum of our existence."

The River Knows No Fear

"A river does not question the boulders in its path; it flows around them. Be like the river—let obstacles shape you, not stop you."

The River and the Mountain

"The river does not doubt whether it will reach the ocean; it simply flows. The mountain does not question whether it stands tall; it simply is. Only the human mind, blessed with thought, is cursed with hesitation. Trust, and flow like the river."

The River's Wisdom

"A river does not resist the pull of gravity. It flows, carves valleys, shapes mountains, and reaches the ocean. Life is the same—when we surrender to truth, we do not lose ourselves; we become something greater."

The Sanctuary Within

"Happiness is not a gift you give away to be validated; it is a sanctuary you build within, untouched by the fleeting expectations of others."

The Seed of Inner Joy

"Chasing everyone's happiness is like trying to catch the wind—elusive and endless. But finding joy within yourself is planting a seed that blossoms unconditionally."

The Shadow and the Flame

"A candle does not fear the darkness; it simply shines. Let courage be your flame, and watch fear shrink into nothing but a passing shadow."

The Shadow and the Sun

"The shadow chases you only when you walk away from the sun. Turn toward the light, and even the darkest fears will fall behind you."

The Shadow of the Mind

"Doubt is like a shadow—it grows when we turn away from the light. Walk towards the light of faith, and the shadow will shrink behind you."

The Silence Between Words

"It is not always what is said that shapes us, but the silence in between—the unspoken truths, the quiet understanding, the spaces where love breathes without sound."

The Silence Between Words

"True understanding is not found in the noise of endless thought, but in the quiet space where wisdom speaks."

The Source of Love

"Love is not a commodity to be obtained, but the very essence that flows through us when we let go of all expectations and attachments."

The Spirit's Light

"When you seek truth, do not look with your eyes; look at the light of your spirit."

The Strength of Serenity

"Serenity is not found in the absence of chaos, but in the quiet strength to remain steady amidst it. Balance is the harmony of the heart when it aligns with life's rhythm."

The Strength of Softness

"The storm may break the oak, but it cannot uproot the grass. Do not mistake gentleness for weakness; the soft endure where the rigid shatter."

The Strength of Surrender

"A tree that refuses to bend will break in the storm, but one that sways with the wind remains standing. Strength is not resistance, but the ability to move with life."

The Strength of Water

"The river never wars with the rock; it flows around it, shaping it with time. True strength is not in resistance, but in adaptability."

The Thread of Destiny

"Fate is not a chain that binds, nor a map that dictates. It is a thread woven by choice and chance—hold it lightly, and weave with wisdom."

The Timing of the Universe

"The universe does not rush, yet everything is accomplished in perfect timing."

The Uncarved Path

"A sculptor does not see a block of stone—he sees the masterpiece hidden within. Trust that your path is unfolding, even when it seems unfinished."

The Unseen Battle

"The greatest war is not fought with swords, but within the soul. Conquer the doubts within, and no force in the world can defeat you."

The Vision of Unconditional Love

"To love unconditionally is to see beyond the surface and recognise the divine in all things."

The Weight of Forgiveness

"To forgive is not to forget, nor to excuse—it is to unshackle the soul from the past. The first prisoner freed is always yourself."

The Weight of Silence

"A thousand words cannot heal what a moment of true silence can reveal."

The Weight of Silence

"The deepest truths are not found in the noise of the world but in the silence between heartbeats. Listen—not to words, but to the spaces where they fade, and you will hear the whispers of eternity."

The Weight of Silence

"Truth does not always roar; sometimes, it arrives in silence, waiting for a heart willing to listen."

The Weight of Unspoken Truths

"Silence may keep the peace, but it does not heal the wound. Speak with wisdom, for unspoken truths turn into unseen chains."

The Weight of an Unseen Tear

"The heaviest burdens are not the ones we carry in our hands, but the ones we hold in our hearts. A tear unseen, a sigh unheard—these are the quiet weights that shape the soul."

The Weight of the Past

"Guilt is not the voice of wisdom—it is the echo of the past refusing to let go. Do not mistake its heaviness for truth."

The Whisper of the Wind

"The wind does not need approval to blow, nor the sun to shine. Why then do you seek permission to be yourself?"

The Wings of Freedom

"The weight of pleasing everyone will break your wings, but the lightness of pleasing yourself will set your spirit free."

Truth

The Soul's Balm: "Deception may bruise the heart, but the revelation of truth is the balm that heals and enlightens the soul."

Truth in the Fragile Stillness

"In the fragile stillness between each breath, we find the most profound truths—the ones that shape us, define us, and guide us toward our highest self."

Truths Found in Trials

"Life's greatest challenges carve paths to our deepest truths. It is in the storms we find resilience, in the failures we uncover wisdom, and in the pain we discover the boundless capacity to rise again."

Twists That Shape Triumph

"The path to your dreams is seldom straight, but every twist and turn shapes the resilience within you. It is through perseverance that the impossible transforms into reality."

Wisdom Through Falsehoods

"Do not lament the moments lost to falsehoods; instead, celebrate the wisdom gained when the truth finally reveals itself."

Wisdom in the Ordinary

"Wisdom is not the accumulation of knowledge but the ability to see the eternal in the ordinary."

"Harmony with the Ocean

"The ocean of life will toss and turn, but mastery lies in finding harmony with its motions; for it's through the act of swimming that we discover our resilience, courage, and peace within."

"Strength in the Tides

"In the boundless ocean of life, the currents may pull you down, the waves may break over you, but true strength is the ability to rise, adapt, and flow, embracing the rhythm of the tides."

The Power of Kindness

Spreading Compassion and Love

"One act of compassion is never small—it echoes. Through a smile, a listening ear, a helping hand, you become a living thread in the fabric of someone's healing."

- *Shree Shambav*

A Legacy of Truth

"The weight of truth is not a burden—it is a gift, an inheritance that asks only for courage to carry it. In revealing it, we do not break; we rebuild."

A Quiet Poem of Life

"You are the universe's quiet poem, unfolding in the rhythm of your breath; your mere presence is a testament to life's splendour."

Awareness

The Light in Darkness: "Awareness is the flame that dispels the shadows of ignorance; with it, even the most entrenched struggles can become pathways to clarity and wisdom."

Beyond the Horizon

"The journey is never about reaching the treasure—it is about becoming the one who no longer needs it."

Bridges of Empathy

"Listening with your heart builds bridges over chasms that words alone cannot cross."

Coming Home to Emptiness

"He returned not to find home, but to learn that home was never a place—it was the people, and they were gone."

Cracks of Light

"The wounds we carry may never fully fade, but it is through the cracks they leave behind that the light of love and forgiveness shines the brightest, showing us the way forward."

Empathy in Conflict

"Conflict is not the absence of empathy, but the inability to see beyond our own perspectives. Only empathy can dissolve the walls we create between each other."

Empathy's Healing Power

"Empathy is the silent power that allows us to see through another's pain, to walk beside them in their journey, and to heal together."

Empathy's Transformative Role

"Empathy turns disagreement into dialogue, isolation into connection, and difference into shared understanding."

Liberation Through Virtue

"Replacing harmful habits in speech is not about restraint but about liberation—freeing your words to heal rather than harm."

Listening as Love

"To truly listen is to offer the greatest gift—to hold space for someone's soul to speak."

Listening with Heart and Mind

"When we listen with both heart and mind, we don't just hear; we absorb, we understand, and we respond with kindness."

Love Beyond Distance

"True love is not measured by how close two souls stand, but by how deeply they remain within each other, even in absence."

Nurturing Connections

"In the garden of relationships, virtuous communication is the sunlight that nurtures growth and the rain that mends the cracks."

On Brokenness and Becoming

"We are not shattered to remain broken; we are broken to let the light enter, to be remade into something even the universe will envy."

On Forgiveness

"To forgive is not to erase the wound but to stitch it with threads of love. The scar remains, not as a mark of pain, but as a testament to the strength it took to heal."

On Love Beyond Time

"There are souls we meet in lifetimes we do not remember, yet we recognise them in the way our hearts break when they leave."

On Love's Resilience

"Love is not fragile—it bends, it breaks, and yet it endures. In its quiet strength, it rebuilds what hatred sought to destroy."

On Love's Silence

"The deepest love is not always spoken—it lingers in the spaces between words, in the pauses where a heart dares not confess."

On Redemption

"Redemption is not found in the absence of mistakes but in the courage to confront them, the wisdom to learn from them, and the grace to rise above them."

On Time's Mercy

"Time does not heal, it only teaches us how to carry what was never meant to be left behind."

On the Fragility of Truth

"The truth is not always what we say—it is also what we hide, what we whisper only to the night, what we bury in silence."

On the Soul's Memory

"Some places remember us long after we have left, just as some hearts hold our presence long after we are gone."

On the Weight of Absence

"The heaviest thing a heart can hold is not loss, but the presence of someone who is no longer there."

Planting Trust

"Words are not just sounds; they are seeds. Plant them with care, and they will grow into trust, love, and understanding."

Promises

"Some promises are not meant to be fulfilled in this life, but in the quiet spaces between hearts, where love never fades."

Seeds of Connection

"Kind words are the seeds of connection; when sown with intention, they blossom into trust and understanding."

The Alchemy of Pain

"The fire that destroys can also forge. Pain does not merely break you; it reshapes you, if only you let it carve wisdom where there was once only sorrow."

The Alignment of Words and Purpose

"Words are not just a reflection of our thoughts; they are the embodiment of our values. Pausing before speaking allows us to align our words with our purpose, creating communication that heals, connects, and elevates."

The Anchor of Love

"Family isn't about perfection or wholeness; it's about standing beside each other even when the ground beneath us crumbles. In the fractures of our hearts, love becomes the anchor that holds us steady."

The Art of Letting Go

"To hold on is to fear the unknown, but to let go is to trust the journey. Like autumn leaves surrendering to the wind, find freedom in releasing what no longer serves your soul."

The Art of Letting Go

"To hold on to the past is to grip a blade; the tighter you cling, the deeper the wound. Freedom is not in forgetting, but in learning to carry memories with open hands."

The Battlefield Within

"The greatest war we face is not with the world outside, but within the quiet corridors of our mind—where our fears, doubts, and desires reside as adversaries, waiting to be understood and transcended."

The Death of the Old Self

"The greatest act of courage is to let go of who you were, not because you forget the pain but because you choose to honour the strength that grew from it."

The Echo of Time

"Memories are not chains that bind us to the past, but echoes that remind us we were once deeply alive. Let them guide you forward, not hold you back."

The Echoes of Kindness

"A single act of kindness is like a pebble cast into a still lake—its ripples reach shores unseen, touching lives in ways we may never know."

The Echoes of Loss

"Grief is not the absence of love but the presence of it in unbearable silence. It lingers in unspoken words, in empty spaces, in the echoes of what once was."

The Empathy Pause

"Empathy begins in the pause before we speak, where the heart chooses kindness over impulse, and understanding over judgment."

The Essence of Humanity

"We may see people in every corner of the world, but it is the rare soul that embodies the essence of humanity—an openness to love, serve, and connect with others in their deepest need."

The Final Lesson

"In the end, all that remains of a man are his choices, his kindness, and the love he dared to give."

The Fire of Anger

"Anger is not the villain—it is the mirror, showing us the wounds we've hidden too long. To wield it wisely is to turn fire into light, and to let it burn wildly is to destroy the bridge to healing."

The Fragility of Illusions

"A house built on illusions will always crumble under the weight of truth. But in the rubble, you find what truly matters—the people who stay, not for what you've built, but for who you are."

The Fragility of Moments

"A lifetime is not lost in years, but in moments—moments missed, moments unspoken, moments unlived."

The Freedom of Truth

"Honest words may feel heavy in the moment, but they carry the lightness of a free and unburdened soul."

The Ghosts We Carry

"Some people never leave us, not because they stay, but because we carry them in the empty spaces they once filled."

The Gift of Presence

"The greatest gift you can offer someone in their time of struggle is not advice, but your full presence, listening with your heart wide open."

The Heart of Empathy

"Empathy is not merely a feeling, but a deep understanding that connects us beyond words, allowing us to see the world through another's heart."

The Heart of Humanity

"Humanity is not merely the presence of people, but the presence of compassion, kindness, and understanding that transcends the crowd."

The Home

"A village is not just land and walls—it is laughter echoing through the streets, the warmth of familiar faces, and the stories woven into its soil. When those are gone, what remains is only a shell of what once was."

The Home That Time Forgot

"We chase the past like a mirage, only to find that time has rewritten its script, and the home we seek exists only in our memories."

The Illusion of Treasure

"Many spend their lives chasing gold, only to realise the true treasure was the journey itself."

The Journey to Liberation

"True liberation is not the absence of struggle but the mastery of it—walking through the storm with a steady heart, anchored in truth, and illuminated by love."

The Journey's True End

"He spent a lifetime chasing a treasure buried in the earth, only to find that the greatest wealth had always been buried in his heart."

The Last Promise

"Love does not count years, nor measure distances—it simply waits, unwavering, even when the body can no longer endure the weight of time."

The Legacy of Speech

"Our words are echoes that linger far beyond their utterance, shaping the world and the memories we leave behind."

The Letter's Light

"Words, written with love, have the power to outlive their author. They become whispers in the dark, guiding the lost and reminding the weary that they were never forgotten."

The Light Within the Ruins

"Even in the wreckage, beauty remains. A shattered soul is not an ending—it is a mosaic waiting to be pieced into something more profound than before."

The Light of Your Being

"The beauty of your existence lies not in what you do, but in the undeniable truth that you are here, a unique light in the vast expanse of being."

The Masterpiece of You

"Your existence is a masterpiece, woven from the threads of stardust and infinite possibilities—a beauty that requires no validation."

The Mirror of Empathy

"To listen with empathy is to offer a mirror, not to reflect what we think, but to reflect what the other needs to see in themselves."

The Mirror of Speech

"Your words are mirrors reflecting not just how you see the world but how you wish the world to see you."

The Mirror of Words

"Every word you choose reflects not just what you feel but who you are becoming—speak with the intention to build, not break."

The Mirror of the Heart

"He sought the truth in distant lands, only to find it staring back at him in his reflection."

The Path of the Seeker

"The weight of gold can build empires, but the weight of wisdom builds eternity. The true seeker walks not toward wealth, but toward awakening."

The Pause of Clarity

"A pause before speaking is a moment of clarity—a chance to align your words with your values."

The Power of Words

"Every word we speak is a brushstroke on the canvas of life—choose them with care, for they paint the masterpiece of our relationships."

The Power of Words

"Every word we speak is a seed sown in the garden of our relationships—choose your words with care, and watch trust, understanding, and love bloom where once there were thorns."

The Price of Love

"Love is not the absence of pain; it is the courage to stand amidst it, to see someone's broken pieces and choose to hold them anyway. It is not what mends the cracks—it is the gold that fills them, making the broken whole again."

The Price of Power

"He conquered lands, built empires, and amassed riches, yet the only thing he could not buy back was time."

The Quiet Between Us

"Sometimes, love isn't in the words we say but in the silences we share—spaces where forgiveness and understanding quietly grow."

The Quiet Power of Empathy

"In a world where everyone is shouting to be heard, empathy is the quiet voice that listens and builds bridges where there were walls."

The Ripple of Change

"The smallest shift in how we speak can ripple through a relationship, transforming tension into connection and silence into harmony."

The Shadow of Guilt

"Guilt is a thief, not of the past but of the present. It turns mirrors into windows of regret, reflecting not who you are but the mistakes you believe define you."

The Silence Within

"True wisdom is not in the words we speak, but in the silence, we honour before them."

The Silent Oath

"Sometimes, promises are not spoken aloud but carried in the quiet resolve of our hearts. To protect, to heal, to love—these are the silent oaths that shape the bond of a family."

The Silent Sacrifice

"Parents give everything they have, not for recognition, but for the silent hope that their children will remember them when they have nothing left to give."

The Symphony of Kindness

"Each kind word is a note in the symphony of humanity, transforming discord into harmony."

The Tapestry of Connection

"Empathy is the thread that ties the heart to the mind, creating a tapestry of connection, understanding, and love."

The Unfinished Symphony

"Life does not stop when dreams shatter; it merely composes a different melody. The music of the soul never truly ends—it only finds new ways to be heard."

The Unspoken Goodbyes

"The deepest grief is not in the words we say, but in the words we never got the chance to speak."

The Weight of Forgiveness

"Forgiveness is not the absolution of wrongdoing but the liberation of the soul from the chains of anger. To forgive is to reclaim your peace, even when the wound still bleeds."

The Weight of Gossip

"To gossip is to throw shadows on someone else's light, forgetting that it dims your own."

The Weight of Redemption

"Redemption isn't about erasing the past—it's about facing it, raw and unfiltered, and choosing to become someone better. It's the heaviest weight one can carry, but it's also the only one that sets you free."

The Weight of Redemption

"Redemption isn't about erasing the past—it's about facing it, raw and unfiltered, and choosing to become someone better. It's the heaviest weight one can carry, but it's also the only one that sets you free."

The Weight of Silence

"Some wounds do not bleed, but they echo in silence. And in that silence, we either break or we listen—until we learn to heal."

The Weight of Silence

"Some wounds do not bleed, yet they carve the deepest scars. The heaviest pain is often the one carried in silence, unheard but never unfelt."

The Weight of Time

"Time does not ask for permission; it takes what it wants, leaving behind only echoes of what once was."

The Weight of Unspoken Love

"Not all love is meant to be declared. Some remain like an unfinished melody, forever playing in the quiet chambers of the heart."

The Weight of a Whisper

"Sometimes, the most profound lessons are not shouted but whispered in the quiet moments before goodbye—echoing forever in the hearts of those who remain."

The Whisper of Fate

"Destiny does not shout; it whispers. Only those who dare to listen will hear its call. Only those who dare to follow will find its truth."

Through the Cracks

"A family is not perfect, nor is it meant to be. The cracks in our relationships are where forgiveness seeps in, mending us with threads of understanding and love."

Through the Fog of Time

"The past never leaves us; it lingers in the echoes of forgotten laughter, in the scent of a distant memory, in the touch of a ghost that never truly lets go."

Transformative Conversations

"Conversations are not exchanges of words; they are the alchemy of transformation when infused with sincerity, love, and presence."

True Humanity Defined

"In a world full of human beings, it is rare to encounter true humanity, for it is not bound by the flesh but by the heart's capacity to care beyond self."

True Listening

"True listening is not the act of hearing sounds, but of feeling the emotions behind them and responding with compassion."

Wisdom from the Ages

Timeless Insights for Life

"Life may evolve, but the essence of truth remains unchanged. What guided the hearts of generations before us still pulses beneath our choices—love, humility, and grace."

- *Shree Shambav*

A Child's Quiet Wisdom

"Some souls arrive not to learn from the world, but to teach it—small hands offering the wisdom that time often forgets."

A Lantern of Kindness

"To speak with kindness is to offer a lantern to the lost; it illuminates paths unseen and warms the coldest nights."

A Melody of Understanding

"When speech is guided by compassion, it becomes a melody that resonates with the unspoken needs of others."

A Strength, Not a Weakness

"Compassion in speech is not a weakness but a strength; it bridges the chasms that divide us and builds foundations of trust."

Becoming Love

"Love is not something you give or receive; it is the essence you become when you remember you are one with all."

Beyond the Veil of Time

"We are not bound by the minutes that pass but by the moments that live forever within us."

Echoes of Loss

"Grief is not a wound that heals with time but a shadow that grows quieter, following you into every dawn. It does not leave you; it teaches you how to carry it."

Echoes of the Soul

"When love guides our words, they become echoes of the soul—reaching places where the light of understanding begins to shine."

Harmony in the Duality

"Life is not a choice between roots and wings; it is the art of weaving them together. Only when they coexist can we truly grow and soar."

Inner Peace Through Minimalism

"When we choose less, we open ourselves to more: more peace, more clarity, more connection to our higher purpose."

Justice and the Heart

"True justice is not found in the letters of law, but in the spaces between them. It is not measured in punishment, but in the mercy we dare to show."

Kindness as a Legacy

"True strength is not in shielding yourself from pain, but in allowing kindness to bloom in its shadow, so that others may find shelter under its shade."

Living with Intentionality

"Living with intention is not about doing more, but about doing less—focusing only on what adds true value to our lives."

On Eternity's Touch

"We are more than flesh and bone—we are the love we leave behind, the stories that outlive us, the light that refuses to dim."

On Gratitude and Redemption

"Gratitude is not a debt to be repaid but a light to be passed forward. It is the language of the soul, whispering that even in our darkest moments, someone believed we were worthy of the dawn."

On Love Beyond Blood

"Family isn't bound by bloodlines but by the courage to open your heart and trust in someone else's goodness, even when life has taught you to doubt."

On the Echoes of the Soul

"We do not vanish when we leave this world—we become echoes in the wind, whispers in the light, songs in the hearts that loved us."

On the Weight of Acceptance

"To accept love is the bravest act of all, for it demands that we see ourselves not through the shattered glass of our past but through the eyes of someone who sees only our worth."

Purpose Beyond Opportunity

A reminder that true fulfilment lies in pursuing what aligns with one's heart, not just external accolades.

Ripples of Change

"Words infused with intention are like prayers whispered into the wind—they reach far beyond what we can see, creating ripples of change."

Roots and Wings

"A family's strength lies not in how tightly it holds its members but in how freely it allows them to grow. Letting go doesn't mean losing; it means trusting the roots you've planted."

Sowing Seeds of Peace

"To speak with love is to sow seeds of peace, transforming even the harshest ground into fertile soil for understanding."

The Anchor of Roots

"A tree without roots is a shadow of itself, swaying with every storm. Stay grounded in who you are, and no wind will uproot your spirit."

The Art of Breaking

"A heart that has never broken has never truly lived, for it is in the fractures that light enters, in the shattering that we are reborn."

The Art of Harmony

"True harmony isn't the absence of conflict; it's the ability to weave every discord into a melody so profound that even the dissonance finds its place."

The Art of Letting Go

"To release the weight of unnecessary possessions is to find the freedom to carry only what is essential for the soul's journey."

The Balance of Light and Shadow

"Happiness and sorrow are not opposites but partners in the dance of life. It is in the shadow of loss that the light of love burns brighter, revealing what truly matters."

The Chains We Do Not See

"Not all prisons have walls. Some are built from unspoken regrets, some from the fear of change, and the worst of all—from the lies we tell ourselves to avoid the truth."

The Chains of Power

"A man who seeks power believes he is climbing toward freedom, but with each step, he forges new chains—chains of expectation, of fear, of endless hunger. Until one day, he looks back and realises he has not ascended—he has merely built his own prison."

The Cleansing of the Mind

"A decluttered space leads to a decluttered mind, and a decluttered mind leads to a life of focused intention and deep peace."

The Cost of Revenge

"Revenge is a fire that promises warmth but leaves only ashes. You may burn your enemy, but in the end, you will find yourself standing in ruins."

The Courage to Say No

"To say no to distractions is to say yes to our deepest desires, our truest calling, and our most authentic self."

The Courage to Simplify

"Simplicity is an act of courage—it requires us to look inward and face the things we have been holding onto that no longer serve us."

The Echo of Betrayal

"Betrayal does not come from an enemy's blade but from a friend's whisper. A stranger's hatred wounds the skin; a loved one's deception wounds the soul."

The Echo of Lost Footsteps

"Every road we walk leaves an imprint, even if we never return. Some places remember us, even when we forget them."

The Echo of Us

"In the end, we are all just echoes—of love, of light, of something far greater than ourselves."

The Echoes of Kindness

"A single act of kindness ripples through time, touching lives in ways even the giver may never see."

The Essence of Gratitude

"Gratitude is the key that unlocks the door to abundance—when we give thanks for what we already have, we realise that we need less to be content."

The Eternal Doorway

"Each moment is a doorway to the eternal; step through with awareness, and you will find the infinite waiting."

The Eternal Return

"Every ending is a doorway, every departure a return—love always finds its way home."

The Final Destination

"In the end, all roads lead not to a place, but to a person—the one we were always meant to become."

The Flight of the Spirit

"To rise, we must first fall; to fly, we must first break; to be free, we must first surrender."

The Freedom of Non-Attachment

"Freedom is not in having everything, but in being free from the need for anything."

The Gift of Presence

"To simplify life is to be present in every moment, fully aware of the beauty and grace that already surround us."

The Hands of Time

"Some moments last forever—not because time stops, but because the heart refuses to let them go."

The Heart That Heals

"A heart that listens with empathy crafts words that heal; in the quietness of understanding, love finds its voice."

The Illusion of Power

"A throne may command obedience, but it cannot command love. A crown may weigh heavy, but it cannot grant wisdom. Power is not the chains we place on others, but the ones we unknowingly place upon ourselves."

The Inner Knowing

"The path to wisdom is not in accumulating knowledge but in surrendering to the knowing already within you."

The Journey Home

"We spend our lives searching for something—only to realise that what we seek has always been within us."

The Journey Within

"A traveler may cross a thousand lands, but if he does not journey within, he remains forever lost."

The Language of the Soul

"Not all words are spoken. Some are written in the way we look at each other, in the way we hold on, in the way we say goodbye without ever truly leaving."

The Light That Remains

"Even after the stars burn out, their light continues to travel. Even after people leave, their love lingers in the spaces they once filled."

The Light Within Darkness

"Even in the depths of despair, the smallest spark of love can ignite a fire, illuminating paths you thought were lost to the darkness forever."

The Light of Renewal

"Even after the fiercest storm, the sun does not ask for permission to rise—it simply does, illuminating all that remains and whispering, 'Begin again.'"

The Measure of Success

"Success is not the wealth we accumulate but the love we leave behind, the wisdom we pass on, and the lives we heal when the world feels broken."

The Mirage of Desire

"Chasing after a dream without knowing its meaning is like drinking salt water—each sip only deepens the thirst."

The Mirage of Influence

"Influence is like a river—those who control it believe they own its course, but they are merely its passengers. The river flows for no man, and those who drink deeply from it often find their thirst only grows."

The Mirror of Second Chances

"Darpan wasn't just a child seeking refuge—he was a reflection of all they could be if they chose courage over fear, love over grief. In his eyes, they found not just the past they mourned, but the future they dared to hope for."

The Mirror of Truth

"The greatest treasure is not buried beneath the earth, but reflected in the eyes of a man who has truly understood himself."

The Music of Existence

"Every heartbeat is a note, every breath a lyric—together, we compose the song of existence."

The Music of Longing

"The songs we cherish are not just melodies; they are the voices of our own longing, calling us home to something we lost."

The Ocean Within

"The soul is like the sea—calm on the surface, raging in the depths, always reaching for the shore it may never touch."

The Paradox of Power

"The strongest man is not the one who conquers others, but the one who resists the temptation to rule them."

The Paradox of Trust and Power

"A man in power must choose: to be feared or to be trusted. But fear is a blade that cuts both ways, and trust is a bridge that, once burned, may never be rebuilt. To have both is an illusion, and to have neither is to stand alone in a kingdom of shadows."

The Path to Spiritual Clarity

"The journey of spiritual growth begins with simplicity—by shedding the unnecessary, we find the clarity needed to hear the whisper of our soul."

The Power of Gentle Words

"The gentlest words have the power to calm storms within others; they are the soft rains that quench parched hearts."

The Power of Simplicity

"Simplicity is the gateway to clarity—when we clear the clutter of our lives, we make space for our truest selves to emerge."

The Price of Freedom

"A man is not free because he has no chains; he is free only when his heart does not long for what enslaves him."

The Quiet Strength of Love

"True resilience is not in never breaking but in choosing to rebuild, brick by fragile brick, with love as your mortar and hope as your scaffold."

The Rhythm of Goodbye

"Every goodbye is a song—a melody of what was, a harmony of what remains, and a silence that sings long after the music fades."

The Ripple Effect of Simplicity

"When one person lives with intention and simplicity, they ripple waves of transformation that touch everyone they encounter."

The River of Light

"No matter how lost you feel, the current of love will always find its way back to you."

The Roots of Legacy

"A tree may stretch its branches to the skies, but its strength lies in the unseen roots that hold it steady. Legacy is not what we leave behind—it is what we nurture in the hearts we touch."

The Sacred Rhythm

"Each breath is an unspoken dialogue between the finite and the infinite, a sacred rhythm binding you to the cosmos."

The Sacredness of Less

"In the quiet space of less, we discover the sacredness of everything: our relationships, our thoughts, and the very air we breathe."

The Silent Bridge Between Words and Actions

"Integrity is the silent bridge between words and actions, where trust finds its home and truth speaks without a need for persuasion."

The Silent Echo

"Some truths are not spoken but felt—like a whisper in the wind, like the shadow of a memory that refuses to fade."

The Silent Symphony

"Some stories are not written in words but in the quiet symphony of a soul unspoken."

The Silent Victory

"Not all battles end with swords drawn; some are won in silence, when a man chooses wisdom over war."

The Sound of Forever

"In the end, we are not our names, nor our bodies, nor our days on this earth. We are echoes—of love, of light, of something infinite."

The Test of True Freedom

"A man is not free when he follows rules without question. Nor is he free when he breaks them without thought. True freedom lies in knowing when to uphold, when to challenge, and when to rewrite the laws of his own life."

The Threads of Family

"A family isn't always built on blood. Sometimes, it's woven from threads of shared pain, quiet resilience, and the stubborn belief that love, no matter how broken, can still bind us together."

The True Abundance

"Abundance is not measured by the things we possess, but by the peace we experience when we let go of what no longer serves us."

The True Value of Time

"Time is our most precious resource; when we simplify, we gain more time for the things that truly nourish our soul."

The Unfinished Chapter

"Not all stories find their ending, but that does not mean they are incomplete. Some love exists beyond the pages, in the spaces between what was written."

The Weight of Longing

"There is a love that never fades, a longing that never dies, a presence that lingers even in absence."

The Weight of Love

"Sometimes, the heaviest burdens we carry are not the ones that break us, but the ones that remind us of what we've lost. And yet, love demands we carry them, not to mourn forever, but to honour what was and what can still be."

The Weight of an Empty Soul

"A man can fill his pockets with gold, yet if his soul remains empty, he is still a beggar in the grand marketplace of life."

The Whisper of Time

"Time does not steal youth; it merely reveals the face that was always hiding beneath it."

The Whispers Within

"The soul does not scream; it whispers. Only in silence can you hear its deepest truths."

Through the Fog

"Not all paths are meant to be seen—some must be felt, one uncertain step at a time."

Unseen Sacrifices

"True loyalty isn't loud or boastful; it's the quiet voice that says, 'I will stand by you, even if you never notice me.'"

Wings of Purpose

"Dreams are not meant to escape the earth but to soar high enough to bring back the sky. Ambition without purpose is like a bird with wings but no direction."

Words Carry Energy

"Every word carries energy—let it be a balm to the wounded, a light to the weary, and a blessing to those who hear."

Words Felt, Not Just Heard

"The words we speak are not just heard but felt; when rooted in love, they leave a warmth that lingers in the hearts of others."

Words as Reflections of the Soul

"Our words are reflections of our inner world; to speak with love is to reveal the beauty of the soul within."

"Shadows Without Light"

"Words without integrity are like shadows without light—fleeting, hollow, and ultimately forgotten."

"The Courage to Remain Whole"

"To live with integrity is to carry the courage to remain whole, even in a world that often rewards compromise."

"The Echo of Harmony"

"When our actions echo our words, we create a harmony that resonates far beyond mere speech, building bridges of trust that cannot be shaken."

"The Silent Guardian"

"Integrity is the silent guardian of trust, ensuring that even in the absence of explanation, our character speaks for itself."

Life Coach and Philanthropist

Shree Shambav is the visionary founder of the Shree Shambav Ayur Rakshita Foundation (www.shambav-ayurrakshita.org). He founded this institution with a lofty goal: to recognise human identity across gender, ethnicity, and nationality. Through this organisation, he wants to assist all communities in realising their full potential and the intrinsic beauty of life.

Shree Shambav, a Life Coach, is dedicated to supporting people on their journeys of self-discovery and empowerment. He assists people in discovering who they are, determining what inspires and drives them, and overcoming limiting ideas. His approach clarifies what one wants in life, assisting people through goal-setting and a step-by-step process for achieving them. He empowers people to make deliberate and responsible decisions, allowing them to identify their blind spots and evolve as individuals via the use of numerous strategies and tools.

The foundation's bold, uncompromising, and compassionate ventures are always aimed at initiating the "Inner Transformation" process. They focus on spiritual growth, personal growth, and self-healing while emphasising that true progress lies in "Inclusive Growth and Co-existence." This philosophy drives all their initiatives, encouraging a holistic approach to development and well-being.

Under Shree Shambav's leadership, the foundation has launched several impactful movements:

Shree Shambav Green Movement: This mission is to create a healthy, green, and clean earth through responsible water conservation and greening initiatives. The movement strives to make the world a green paradise by encouraging sustainable living and environmental responsibility.

Shree Shambav Vidya Vedhika (Vizhuthugal): This project aims to help students and children by offering training, books, stationery, and uniforms. It aims to provide the next generation with the tools and resources they need to excel both academically and personally.

Shree Shambav and his foundation exemplify the spirit of compassion, transformation, and inclusive growth via their work, which has a profound impact on individuals and communities around the world. His work exemplifies the power of acknowledging and nourishing the human spirit, creating a world in which everyone can reach their full potential and appreciate the beauty of life.

TESTIMONIALS

Journey of Soul - Karma - "We die in our twenties and are buried at eighty." Remember that nothing can stop someone who refuses to be stopped. "Most people do not fail; they simply give up." Shree Shambav deserves full credit. It allowed me to sit and consider what I might miss out on in life. The author has delved into every aspect of our daily lives. How can a seemingly insignificant change in these seemingly insignificant details bring us such joy? The Soul of Journey teaches you the "art of living" as well as the "art of dying."

Twenty + One Series - The rich cultural heritage offered a host in twenty + one short stories with incredible imagination, morals and values prevalent at a given time, influencing how people respond to a crisis or any situation. The author has recreated images with universal values and morals. The plentiful of fascinating from faraway lands would leave the modern play and story writers a cringe. The book supports trust and immeasurable values, instilling hope for the new generations.

Death - "Shree Shambav's 'Death - Light of Life and the Shadow of Death' is an extraordinary masterpiece that delves deep into the profound questions surrounding our existence and mortality. The book's opening statement, 'Nothing ever truly dies; it simply ceases to exist in one form before resuming it in another,' sets the stage for a thought-provoking exploration of death's multifaceted nature. Shambav's remarkable ability to navigate the philosophical complexities of death and our universal fear of it is both enlightening and comforting. This book is a testament to the power of understanding and acceptance."

Whispers of Eternity - "Reading 'Whispers of Eternity' by Shree Shambav was a transformative experience that left me captivated from beginning to end. Each section of this exquisite collection delves into the myriad facets of existence, offering poignant reflections on life, death, and everything in between. Shree Shambav's verses are a testament to the beauty of language and the power of expression, inviting readers to embark on a journey of self-discovery and spiritual awakening. Whether celebrating life's simple joys or grappling with the complexities of human emotion, this book is a timeless companion that speaks to the heart and soul of every reader."

Life Changing Journey Series - "Life Changing Journey Series II Inspirational Quotes" is a remarkable collection that illuminates the path to self-discovery and personal growth. With its inspiring quotes and insightful reflections, this book serves as a beacon of light in a world often shrouded in darkness. Each quote offers wisdom, guidance, and encouragement, reminding readers of their inner strength and resilience. A must-read for anyone seeking inspiration and enlightenment.

Learn To Love Yourself – "A Heartfelt Guide to Authentic Self-Love." "Learn to Love Yourself" invites readers on a transformative journey to embrace their true essence in a world often focused on external validation. Through ten insightful chapters, it gently reveals principles of genuine self-love, guiding readers to deepen their connection with themselves. Beyond surface positivity, it encourages the cultivation of resilient self-acceptance, from embracing one's unique qualities to setting empowering boundaries. With inspiring stories and practical wisdom, this book is a trusted companion on the path to inner peace, fulfilment, and joy, helping readers build lives that reflect their authentic selves.

The Power of Letting Go – This book has been a gift to my spiritual journey. Shree Shambav's insights into attachment, personal growth cycles, and forgiveness are enlightening. The concept of seven-year cycles resonated with me, helping me understand the natural phases of life. I feel more empowered to let go of what no longer serves me and step into a life of freedom and fulfilment. A truly beautiful read!

A Journey of Lasting Peace – "A Journey of Lasting Peace" feels like a trusted friend guiding you through the maze of self-discovery. The 18 transformative principles are both practical and deeply resonant, addressing everything from gratitude practices to the art of letting go. Each chapter is infused with warmth and wisdom, making it easy to apply the concepts to my life. I particularly appreciated the emphasis on physical health's connection to mental well-being; it served as a wake-up call for me to prioritise my health. This book is an invaluable resource for anyone serious about personal growth!

Astrology Unveiled Series – "Profound, Logical, and Inspiring". What stands out in Astrology Unveiled is the author's dedication to making Vedic astrology logical and approachable. Each concept flows naturally into the next, backed by examples and exercises. The insights into karma and life cycles add a philosophical depth rarely seen in astrology books. Perfect for anyone seeking spiritual growth alongside astrological knowledge!

The Entitlement Trap - "Thought-Provoking and Challenging" The book challenges readers to confront their own sense of entitlement, and that's not easy—but it's essential. The Entitlement Trap doesn't offer a one-size-fits-all approach. Instead, it's a thoughtful, layered examination of how entitlement can limit our growth. The chapter on "Defining Your Own Hill" was particularly impactful, as it pushed me to reconsider which challenges are truly worth pursuing. A thought-provoking read for those willing to do the inner work to create a life they can be proud of.

Whispers of a Dying Soul – "A Soul-Stirring Reflection on Life's Unspoken Truths" **-** *Whispers of a Dying Soul: Unspoken Regrets and Unlived Dreams"* is a deeply moving exploration of the unexpressed emotions and unfulfilled aspirations that shape our lives in ways we often don't realise. This book invites readers to confront the powerful, often hidden impact of regret while guiding them through a journey of introspection and healing. Each page opens a space to reflect on the choices that define us—from moments of unspoken love to neglected passions—offering a gentle reminder to live authentically and courageously.

Whispers of the Soul: A Journey Through Haiku - is a mesmerising collection that speaks directly to the heart. Each haiku is a delicate brushstroke capturing life's fleeting beauty and timeless wisdom, inviting readers into moments of deep reflection and peace. This book is a balm for the soul, guiding us to find meaning in stillness and connection in simplicity. The themes of nature, love, and mindfulness echo universal truths, resonating with quiet, powerful grace. It's a book to be savoured slowly, cherished deeply, and returned to often. Truly, it is a gift for anyone seeking calm and clarity in life's chaos.

Whispers of Silence - Unlocking Inner Power through Stillness by Shree Shambav is a rare gem that beckons readers to pause, reflect, and reconnect with their inner selves. In a world that never stops talking, this book offers a profound exploration of silence—not as a void but as a rich and transformative space.

From the first page, Shree Shambav's writing resonates deeply, blending scientific insights with spiritual wisdom in a way that feels both universal and deeply personal. The author's ability to bridge the tangible and the transcendent makes this book an invaluable guide for anyone navigating the chaos of modern life.

The Power of Words: Transforming Speech, Transforming Lives - The Power of Words is a profound and enlightening guide that has transformed the way I approach communication. Shree Shambav masterfully uncovers the hidden influence of our words on relationships, self-perception, and overall well-being. This book doesn't just teach you how to speak; it inspires mindful communication that fosters connection and trust. The insights on replacing negative patterns like gossip and judgment with kindness and authenticity are truly life-changing. The practical strategies and engaging narratives make it an invaluable resource for personal and professional growth. A must-read for anyone striving to communicate with intention, clarity, and compassion. Highly recommended!

The Art of Intentional Living: Minimalism for a Life of Purpose - "The Art of Intentional Living is a refreshing guide to finding clarity in a cluttered world. With practical wisdom and profound insights, it inspires you to simplify, prioritise, and live with purpose. A must-read for anyone seeking balance and fulfilment."

ACKNOWLEDGEMENTS

My grandfathers, grandmothers, mothers, fathers, aunts, uncles, neighbours, sisters, brothers, friends, and teachers, they poured in endless moral stories, retellings of Ramayana, Mahabharata, Puranas, Upanishads, and so on.

My teachers, neighbours, and kindred souls. Who provided us with a stage to perform wonderful Puranic stories and were gracious enough to acknowledge our efforts.

The artists and translators of epics have served as a source of inspiration, invigorating our spirits, making these works accessible, and enabling us to grasp the profound depths and deeper dimensions they contain.

I also cherish the stimulating conversations I had with my wonderful mothers, Punitha Muniswamy and Uma Devi.

Our family's youngest member, Aadhya, who always overwhelmed me with questions, inspired this book.

I would likewise prefer to express gratitude to Mr Sivakumar, Mrs Roopa Sivakumar, Mr Akshaya

Rajesh, Ms Akshatha Rajesh, Ms Apeksha Prabhu, Mr Akanksh Prabhu, Mr Nikash Sarasambi, and Mrs Spoorthi Nikash for their valuable inputs.

I must thank Mr Rajesh, Mr Savan Prabhu, Mrs Revathi Rajesh, Mrs Rajani Sarasambi, and Mrs Manju Reshma, who encouraged me and often suggested writing a book. Their unwavering belief that I had something valuable to offer kept me going during my writing sessions.

Love you all,

Shree Shambav

www.shambav.org

shreeshambav@gmail.com

BOOKS BY – AUTHOR

Journey of Soul - KARMA

"Journey of Soul – Karma" is a heartfelt exploration of life's profound truths in our increasingly complex world. Addressing challenges, inequalities, and the quest for meaning, this book brings the timeless concept of Karma into focus. It emphasises Karma not merely as philosophy, but as a guiding principle for our daily lives, inspiring us to walk a path of integrity and purpose. Through this journey, readers gain insights into how actions shape destinies, encouraging a life aligned with truth and compassion. It's a beacon for those seeking a deeper, more fulfilled existence.

Death - Light of Life and the Shadow of Death

In *Light of Life and the Shadow of Death*, the enigma of mortality is approached with clarity and compassion. Death is an inevitable certainty, yet it casts a lingering shadow of fear over our lives, stirring grief and despair as we strive to prolong our time on earth. This profound work examines the fate of departed souls and the heavy emotions we attach to loss. Yet, it offers a path toward accepting death and finding peace amid life's uncertainties. Exploring our origins, ethical values, and purpose, it unveils the sustaining truth of existence. The shadow of death, though daunting, is reframed as a shared, universal experience—one that calls us to confront our deepest fears with wisdom and grace.

Whispers of Eternity 150 Plus - A Symphony of Soulful Verses

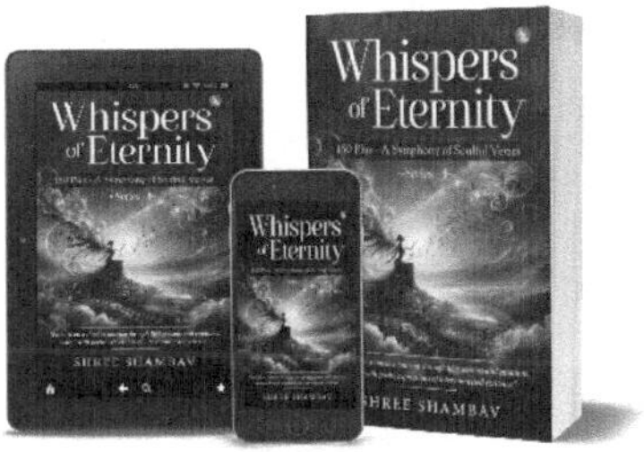

Step into the soul-stirring world of *Whispers of Eternity* by Shree Shambav, a collection of over 150 poems that capture the essence of the human experience. Divided into sections like "Through the Seasons," "Whispers of Hope," and "Threads of Unity," the book journeys through life's phases, emotions, and the universal connections that bind us all. Shree Shambav's verses touch upon nature, love, and spirituality, inspiring readers to find beauty in the everyday. Each poem is a finely crafted reflection, rich with insight and depth. *Whispers of Eternity* invites readers to pause, reflect, and embark on a timeless journey through the landscapes of the heart and soul.

Life Changing Journey Series I and II

In Life Changing Journey - 365 Inspirational Quotes Series I, Shree Shambav curates a powerful collection of 365 original quotes across fourteen chapters, each crafted to touch the heart of our daily lives. More than a simple compilation, this series speaks directly to personal experiences with wisdom and depth. Quotes like, "The most beautiful things are unseen but can be felt," echo the quiet beauty of life's intangible moments. Another, "Giving up is easier; holding oneself up is wiser," provides a guiding light in challenging times. Life Changing Journey reveals the transformative power of carefully chosen words, inspiring readers to find strength and new perspectives on their paths. Through Shree Shambav's work, readers are reminded of the wisdom and resilience hidden within each day.

Twenty + One - 21 Short Stories Series I and II

In *Twenty + One - Short Stories*, Shree Shambav brings to life the often-overlooked characters of nature—trees, animals, and mountains—revealing their intrinsic worth beyond mere utility. With poetic personification, he gives voice to these silent beings, some of whom are lucky enough to have names, titles, and rare human protection. Mountains, usually seen as mere landmarks, are depicted with reverence, emphasising their enduring presence. The stories build a bridge between humans and the natural world, showing that pain, grief, and resilience are shared across all forms of life. Shambav invites readers to empathise with the silent struggles of trees and animals, inspiring a fresh perspective on ecology and our responsibility towards the environment. This collection is a call to honour our connection to nature, encouraging readers to foster compassion and respect for all life.

Learn To Love Yourself

Learn to Love Yourself is a powerful invitation to turn inward in a world focused on external validation and superficial measures. Through ten transformative chapters, each offering a key rule for self-love, readers are guided to uncover their inner beauty, cultivate personal strength, and develop a solid foundation of self-acceptance. This journey goes beyond momentary happiness; it's about building an authentic relationship with yourself that fosters resilience, joy, and fulfilment. From embracing your unique qualities and practising compassion to setting boundaries and pursuing what makes you come alive, this book provides essential insights and practical guidance. Let *Learn to Love Yourself* be your trusted companion on this path, inspiring you to unlock the limitless potential within and find true inner peace.

The Power of Letting Go

The Power of Letting Go invites you to release attachments, fears, and expectations, guiding you toward true inner freedom and joy. With deep insights, practical exercises, and timeless wisdom, this book equips you to face life's challenges with resilience and grace. It explores the essence of attachment, embraces the power of seven-year growth cycles, and teaches the art of forgiveness as a key to a fulfilled life. Each chapter brings concepts to life through relatable analogies and real stories, making profound ideas both accessible and engaging. Let this book serve as your beacon for self-discovery and spiritual awakening, helping you navigate uncertainties and unlock your potential for a joyful, meaningful existence.

A Journey of Lasting Peace

A Journey of Lasting Peace is a transformative guide to self-love, inner peace, and personal strength, where Shree Shambav leads readers through 18 powerful principles for discovering their true selves. Each chapter explores vital themes, from the quest for inner peace and the importance of self-awareness to the healing practices of mindfulness and yoga. Through practical strategies, reflective exercises, and heartfelt stories, this book offers a clear roadmap to a more authentic and fulfilling life.

Whether you seek to embrace imperfection, establish healthy boundaries, or reconnect with nature, A Journey of Lasting Peace provides the wisdom to navigate life's challenges and find enduring tranquillity. Perfect for anyone on a journey of self-discovery, this inspiring work gently reminds us that lasting peace starts within.

Astrology Unveiled: Series I and V

Astrology Unveiled: Foundations of Ancient Wisdom invites you to unlock the mysteries of astrology, offering timeless knowledge rooted in the teachings of ancient sages. This comprehensive guide explores fundamental principles like Rashi, Graha, Bhava, and Divisional charts, making it an essential resource for beginners and intermediate students alike.

With logical explanations and practical applications, Shree Shambav skilfully blends ancient insights with modern understanding. Rich in examples, detailed explanations, and engaging exercises, this book serves as an illuminating path to mastering Vedic astrology.

Embark on a transformative cosmic journey, discovering how astrology can unveil your destiny, guide life's choices, and support your spiritual growth.

The Entitlement Trap: Get Over It, Get On It

Are you feeling stuck in a cycle of blame and dissatisfaction? The Entitlement Trap: Get Over It, Get On It offers a transformative path to reclaiming your personal power. This insightful guide helps you break free from the mindset of victimhood and empowers you to take control of your life. Inside, you'll discover how to redefine success, prioritise your true values, and live with purpose. Through practical strategies, you'll learn to embrace simplicity, connect with nature, and leave a lasting legacy. Get ready to shift from powerless to empowered and create a life you love!

Whispers of a Dying Soul: Unspoken Regrets and Unlived Dreams

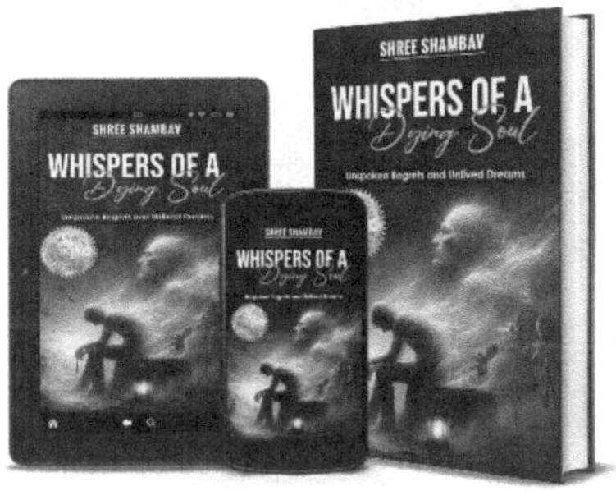

Whispers of a Dying Soul embarks on a profound journey that delves into the silent longings we often carry but seldom express. This powerful exploration uncovers the unspoken emotions that shape our lives—missed opportunities, unfulfilled dreams, and the quest for authenticity. Through heartfelt reflections and transformative insights, this book invites you to confront your regrets and turn them into powerful catalysts for growth and healing.

Whispers of the Soul: A Journey Through Haiku Series I to IV

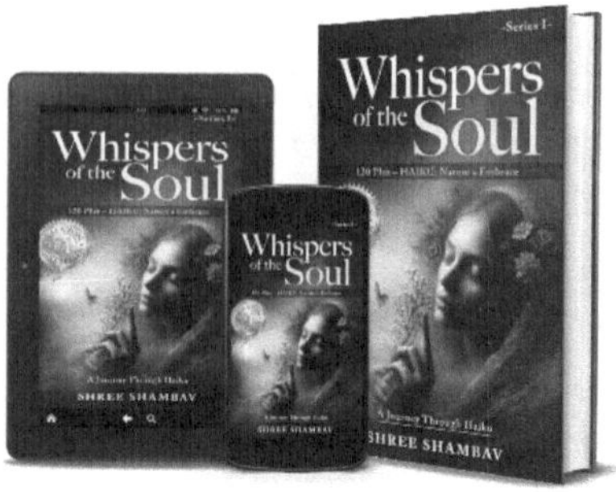

Whispers of the Soul: A Journey Through Haiku is a poetic invitation to pause and rediscover life's hidden beauty. This transformative collection of haikus explores themes of nature, mindfulness, love, and the human journey, offering profound reflections on universal experiences. Divided into five series, the book delves into nature's elegance, the depths of inner stillness, the tenderness of human connection, the passage of life's seasons, and the mysteries beyond the self. Each haiku captures fleeting moments with timeless grace, guiding readers toward peace, self-discovery, and a renewed appreciation for life's simplest wonders. This is more than poetry—it's a soulful journey.

The Power of Words: Transforming Speech, Transforming Lives

The Power of Words: Transforming Speech, Transforming Lives illuminates the profound influence of our everyday language. This book explores how words can heal or harm, connect or divide, urging readers to embrace mindful communication. It delves into the "Sins of Speaking," such as gossip and judgment, while celebrating virtues like honesty, kindness, and authenticity. With practical strategies for transformation and a focus on the art of listening, Shree Shambav offers a roadmap to elevate our conversations. Perfect for both personal growth and professional development, this guide inspires readers to use their words to create peace, foster deeper connections, and lead a life of integrity and purpose.

The Art of Intentional Living: Minimalism for a Life of Purpose

In a world that celebrates more, The Art of Intentional Living invites you to embrace less. This powerful guide explores how minimalism can transform every aspect of your life—your space, your time, and your mind—by removing distractions and focusing on what truly matters.

Through simple yet profound principles, you'll learn to:

- Declutter your physical and digital space
- Prioritise what aligns with your values
- Create time for meaningful connections and experiences
- Cultivate a life of purpose, peace, and clarity

Beyond the Veil: A Journey Through Life After Death

Discover the Eternal Mystery of Life After Death What happens when we die? Is it the end or a transition to something greater? In Beyond the Veil: A Journey Through Life After Death, explore humanity's greatest mystery through the lens of science, spirituality, and philosophy.

From near-death experiences to ancient spiritual teachings, this transformative book bridges the gap between the physical and the infinite, offering profound insights into the afterlife. Whether you're seeking comfort, answers, or inspiration, this journey will deepen your understanding of life, death, and what lies beyond.

Bonds Beyond Blood - Where love builds bridges, and bonds defy blood

Roots and Resilience is a poignant tale set against the quiet rhythm of suburban life, where a family grows strong through love, humility, and sacrifice. But when dreams collide with harsh realities and tragedy strikes, their foundation is shaken, and the true test of their bond begins. At the centre stands a man, torn between honouring his past and forging a future amidst silent struggles within his marriage and the unspoken weight of grief. As the family navigates heartbreak, healing, and the quiet work of rebuilding, they discover that even broken roots can bloom again. This emotional journey is a testament to the resilience of the human spirit, the redemptive power of forgiveness, and the enduring strength found in choosing love—especially when life is at its most imperfect.

A Journey into Spiritual Maturity - 12 Golden Rules for Inner Transformation

In *A Journey into Spiritual Maturity: 12 Golden Rules for Inner Transformation*, Shree Shambav offers a soul-stirring path to self-discovery and inner peace. Blending timeless wisdom with practical tools, this book helps you release attachments, embrace change, and live with intention. Through inspiring stories and guided reflection, you'll learn to nurture self-love, deepen your relationships, and find freedom in authenticity.

Each golden rule is a beacon, illuminating the way toward a more meaningful, compassionate life. It is not just a guide—it's a companion for your soul's awakening. Let this journey lead you home to yourself.

The Inner Battlefield - Overcoming the Enemies of the Mind and Soul

Overcoming the Enemies of the Mind and Soul is a journey into the quiet struggles that shape our lives from within. Through the story of a young seeker and his wise guide, it explores how desire, anger, greed, pride, jealousy, fear, and doubt become obstacles on the path to peace and fulfilment.

With timeless wisdom and practical insights, this book offers tools to confront these inner enemies and transform them into strengths. It is a gentle invitation to rediscover clarity, purpose, and the quiet power of the soul—reminding us that true victory begins within.

The Seeker's Gold - Unlocking Life's Greatest Treasure

The Seeker's Gold follows the journey of a young dreamer, fueled by ambition and the desire for wealth. But as he walks through love, loss, and moments of awakening, he discovers that true riches are not buried in the ground—they're etched in the wisdom life offers through every experience. Encounters with sages, wanderers, and quiet revelations slowly shift his quest from outer treasure to inner truth.

What begins as a pursuit of gold becomes a soulful pilgrimage—challenging his ideas of success, love, and freedom. With each step, he learns that real power lies not in possessing but in understanding. The Seeker's Gold is a transformative tale for those who seek not just more from life, but meaning within it.

9 789334 296525

Printed at Repro India Ltd.